Faith-Building with Preschoolers

Teachers and Parents Together

Linda Prenzlow and Ilene Allinger Candreva

Illustrated by Becky Radtke

Scripture quotations taken from the Holy Bible, New International Version®. NIV®. Copyright © 1973, 1978, 1984 by International Bible Society. Used by permission of Zondervan Publishing House. All rights reserved.

Copyright © 1998 Concordia Publishing House
3558 S. Jefferson Avenue, St. Louis, MO 63118-3968
Manufactured in the United States of America

3   4   5   6   7   8   9   10   07   06   05   04   03   02   01   00

To my son, Alex, who renewed my childlike faith in God. To my husband, Elmer, who provided technical support when my computer screen went blank. To my father-in-law who connected us with the people who could make our dream a reality. And to the Lord—I answered His call.—Linda

Although I wrote the words, many people helped me to create this book. My sons, Kip and Andy, provided the inspiration while my husband, Phil, nourished me with unwavering support. My parents forged a clear path by publishing many books and articles themselves. My former teachers—Dr. Jim Gaudin, Ruth Longman, and Betsy Lubs—nurtured my creative wellspring and developed my technical expertise. But most important, God poured His Holy Spirit into and through my hands, heart, mind, and soul, which spilled out onto this printed page. To Him be the glory! —Ilene

Contents

Introduction

How to Use This Book

It is both a blessing and a challenge to teach children the developmental skills of sharing, following directions, using words, helping, listening, and telling the truth. God is our first teacher and ultimate guide in the task of learning and practicing these skills. This book uses Bible memory verses, child development information, Bible characters/stories, classroom activities, and family-centered projects to teach preschoolers these six basic developmental skills. Activities are designed to address the social, emotional, intellectual, and physical tasks of preschoolers' development.

Each monthly unit will provide ample time for repetition, repetition, and more repetition—the best way for preschoolers to absorb and understand the teaching objectives. Through the **Parent's Letter** and **Family Activities**, classroom lessons will be reinforced at home and children will learn that God's Word is an integral part of their daily lives.

Bible Memory Verse

- **The foundation.** The teaching objective is based on God's Word.

- **Memorize the verse.** If you want the children to value learning this verse, they must see that you have memorized it for your own personal growth. Help the children memorize it through repetition and application.

Teacher's Prayer

- **Copy it** and put it on your desk.

- **Pray it** as you start each day and prepare to teach.

- **Reflect on it.** Gain strength for your task, guidance for modeling God's Word and the teaching objective, and share the joy of your accomplishments with God.

Teaching Objective

- **Identify the developmental skill and Bible character introduced by each unit.**

- **Set your teaching goal and evaluate the children's learning.**

How Children Learn

- **Establish learning expectations** for each child and for your class as a whole.

- **Alter activities and expectations.** Adjust for the children's developmental level. 3-year-olds have very short attention spans; expect to plan many activities for each day. 5-year-olds can focus on a task and have greater interest in creating a product—activities will probably last longer.

- **Activities might not work out as you had planned.** Read this section again and try to adjust your expectations or the activities for a better fit with your classes' developmental level.

- **Each child develops differently.** Do not force a child to do art projects or participate in Circle Time if she is not yet interested. Respect each child's God-given abilities and interests.

- **Preschoolers learn best by doing.** In each of these units, the story is placed *after* the activities. Preschoolers don't have a lot of life experience, so they learn better by doing activities that build upon each other and then tying it all together with a Bible story. The activities become the foundation for the learning and the children will both listen and understand more if the story starts to make sense for them. A 3-year-old has no understanding of Jesus as the Good Shepherd if he hasn't ever seen a sheep and has no idea what a shepherd does to take care of his sheep. If you first show the child the sheep, compare it to animals he already knows, and talk about what it means to care for sheep, the child will be able to make his own connections when the class learns the concept of Jesus as the Good Shepherd.

- **Teach the units in a way that works best for your class.** Feel free to adapt activities, stories, or the order of the unit for your individual class or classes. The key is to help preschoolers understand and apply the concepts of sharing, following directions, using words to communicate, helping, listening, and telling the truth.

Teaching Activities

Decorate the Bible Memory Verse

- **Prepare for the mess.** Most of the Bible memory verses are independent art projects requiring a minimum of adult assistance. (The Bible memory verse in Unit 4 is decorated as a group project and requires adult guidance.) Set up the art projects to minimize the mess; use newspapers, shower curtains, or other coverings for work surfaces and floors.

- **Emphasize process, not product.** Resist the urge to make the pictures "look pretty." Comment on the child's use of color and texture, willingness to try, and

feelings during the experience rather than on the finished product.

- **Encourage appropriate use of art materials.** Show the children how to use the art materials correctly. After giving instructions, let the children enjoy using the paint, glue, scissors, pencils, or other art materials with a minimum of direction. Try to distinguish between a child's inability to use a material and inappropriate use of the material, and provide guidance accordingly. Encourage exploration.

- **Recite the verse.** Ask the children to repeat the verse. Help them memorize the verse, including its reference (book, chapter, and verse).

- **Connect the story.** Help the children retell the Bible story. Prompt when necessary, ask questions, and correct major errors. Make sure the children can identify each unit's teaching objective.

- **Send it home.** Encourage children to display the decorated Bible memory verse in their kitchen, bedroom, or bathroom, wherever they are most likely to see and practice the verse. Or you might want to keep some projects in the classroom on a bulletin board display during the month.

Keeping the Teaching Objective Alive in the Classroom

- **Invest the time.** These projects require some extra work on your part, but they will provide many opportunities for the children to learn and practice each unit's teaching objective in their daily life. These ideas provide continuity for the teaching objective and serve as a focal point for the Bible memory verse, Bible story, and activities.

- **Repeat the unit's teaching objective.** When the children are using this activity, repeat the unit teaching objective often: "please share," "follow directions," "use your words," "please help," "let's listen," and "tell the truth."

Circle-Time Ideas

- **Motion reinforces learning.** Children remember 90 percent of what they do and only 10 percent of what they hear. These activities provide an opportunity to act out the Bible stories, Bible memory verses, and teaching objectives, making the children more likely to incorporate the objectives into their daily lives.
- **Repeat the teaching objective.** Repeat the Bible memory verse and teaching objective often during this activity.
- **Use them more than once.** Repetition increases learning.

Art and Craft Projects

- **Prepare for the mess.**
- **Emphasize process rather than product.**
- **Encourage appropriate use of the art materials.**

Other Activities

- **Use the activities often.**
- **Vary the activities.**
- **Repeat popular activities.** Favorite activities from a unit can be repeated in following units. Find ways to incorporate each unit's teaching objective with previous units' activities. Use these repeated activities as a way of reviewing previous units.

Telling the Story

- **Rehearse the story.** Plan hand gestures, voice changes, eye contact, and other movements that you can use when telling the story. Tell the story with

enthusiasm and excitement. This is God's Word!

- **Assemble all the props.** Practice with the props. Be comfortable with them. They should add to the spoken story, not detract from it.
- **Repeat the unit's teaching objective often.** Preschoolers learn best through repetition.

Parent's Letter and Family Activities

- **Fill in the blanks.** For example, include deadline dates for contributions to the classroom.
- **Sign the letter.**
- **Tell the children what's in the letter.** Stimulate their curiosity about the activities and encourage them to ask their parents to read the letter and try the Family Activities.
- **Send it home.** As simple as this sounds, parents cannot be partners in teaching if they do not know what's happening in the classroom. They need the information and activities contained in this letter to reinforce the teaching objectives at home. (Send Units 1, 3, 4, and 5 home early enough for parents to easily meet deadlines for contributing items to the classroom.)
- **Follow up.** Ask the children if they have done any of the activities with their families. Encourage them to share their experiences. When you meet a child's parents, tell them that you value them as partners with you in their child's education, inspire them to try some of the activities described in each unit, and praise them when they join you in the blessed challenge of teaching developmental skills through God's Word.

Please Share!

Noah Shares Many Things

Bible Memory Verse

The man with two tunics should share with him who has none.
Luke 3:11

Teacher's Prayer

Heavenly Father, You taught Noah's family to share their faith, the task of building the ark, and their temporary home, so also help me to teach the children in my care to share their toys, snacks, and my attention. Give me patience as the children in my care struggle to learn this lesson, and help me recognize their joy at each small success. Amen.

Teaching Objective: Sharing

To help children learn to share, just as Noah's family shared their faith, the task of building the ark, and their temporary home.

Through God's Word and the power of the Holy Spirit, by the end of this unit, the children should be able to:

1. Tell the basic story of Noah and the ark.

2. Repeat the Bible memory verse.

3. Comprehend the teaching objective *sharing*.

4. Show an increased ability to share.

5. Identify a "pair."

Learning to share takes time, practice, and a lot of trust. You can help the children learn to share by first recognizing and remembering how children share at different ages and developmental stages.

How Pre-Schoolers Learn to Share

Age 3: A 3-year-old begins to imitate sharing behavior, but she is still self-focused and unable to understand how her actions affect others. She might understand that she is angry when another child will not share with her, but she is only just beginning to understand how the other child might feel when he doesn't get a turn with a toy. She may share certain toys with certain individuals, under certain circumstances, but does not share consistently. At 3, a child can practice asking permission to play with a toy and practice taking turns. You can help the children learn to share by using the word "share" when requesting, identifying, and praising sharing behavior.

Age 4: A 4-year-old begins to understand *why* it is important to take turns and to share. She begins to want playmates with whom she can share, take turns, fight, and cooperate. Parallel play is replaced by interactive play, a behavior that requires sharing. You can help the children learn to share by encouraging and reinforcing sharing and cooperation so the children's attempts at interactive play and friendships are increasingly successful.

Age 5: A 5-year-old shows a great desire to cooperate; he wants to be good and please others. Two or three 5-year-olds can play together, sharing materials, taking turns, and cooperating to work toward a shared goal. You can help the children learn to share by reinforcing this behavior and moving them toward the more sophisticated form of sharing—shared responsibility. This is a good age to introduce charts that assign classroom responsibilities and a rotation of turn-taking.

Teaching Activities

Decorate the Bible Memory Verse: Stamping Fun

Materials Needed

- Copy of the Bible memory verse (page 13), one for each child
- 3–5 potatoes
- Several colors of tempera paint
- Paper towels to make stamp pads
- Paring knife
- Small bowls to hold paint

What to Do

1. Cut the potatoes in half. On each half, carve an animal's footprint: cat's paw, horse's shoe, deer's hoof, bird's claw, and so on. Be creative—how can you make a snake's "footprint"? (A wavy line, perhaps?) Or an insect's? (Teeny, tiny dots?)

2. Before school starts, set up for this art project as you normally do. Pour the paint on the paper towels to create a stamp pad. Print a few examples to have ready for the children to see.

3. Show the children how to press the footprint stamp on the stamp pad and then on the paper. Help them identify the various footprints.

Teaching Sharing

- Remind the children to share the stamps and the paint, just as Noah had to share with the animals and his family on the ark.

- Stamping can be a difficult technique for young preschoolers; they often smear the paint instead of pressing the stamp on the paper. After showing the children how to stamp, allow them to experiment with the technique. Emphasize the process and not the finished product. The children will be proud of their picture just as Noah was proud when he finished the ark.

Keeping the Teaching Objective Alive in the Classroom—An Ark for Sharing

Materials Needed

- An appliance box or other box large enough to hold several children
- Utility knife
- Brown paint (optional)
- Paintbrush (optional)
- Toy animals (pairs if possible)

What to Do

1. Use the utility knife to cut windows and a door in the appliance box. Paint the exterior of the box to look like Noah's ark. (If you are brave, the children can help with this.) Let dry.

2. Put the ark in your classroom. Fill your ark with animals; the Parent's Letter suggests that the children bring in a labeled stuffed animal or two to load onto this classroom ark. Provisions for the 40-day voyage, animal and people food (pictures or plastic), should be included.

3. Follow your standard classroom practice when introducing this new play space.

Teaching Sharing

- As your preschoolers use the ark, encourage them to share both the space and the animals.

- Once the animals from home are in place, point out to the children how each child is sharing her animal with the class.

Sharin' Shoes: A Circle-Time Game to Teach Sharing

Materials Needed

- Shoes (the ones that the children are wearing, yours, and a pair or two from the dress-up corner)

What to Do

1. During Circle Time, have the children remove their shoes. Put them in a pile in the middle of the circle, along with your shoes and the dress-up shoes.

2. Have the children close their eyes. Mix up the shoes. When the shoes are well mixed, tell the children that they can open their eyes.

3. Call one or two children at a time to find their shoes.

4. Repeat until everyone has had a turn. Your shoes and the dress-up shoes are there to provide a challenge for the last child. Make sure that this child gets to go first when you play this game again.

5. Shoes are an easy way to teach the concept of "pair." Explain that Noah took a pair of each animal into the ark—two of each animal like two of each shoe.

Teaching Sharing

- As the children hand over their shoes, thank them individually for sharing.

- During the game, be an enthusiastic narrator: "It's Elijah's turn. Elijah has found his shoes!" "Jacob is waiting for his turn!" "Wow! I'm so glad that Erin shared her shoes with us!" "Look! Nikki found both of her shoes! Clap for Nikki!" (This will help keep the waiting children involved in the game.) Incorporate the teaching objectives in your narration, "Just like I promised, you got your own shoes back."

Matching Up Dominoes: A Cooperative Game

Materials Needed

- One copy of each page of the Animal Dominoes (pages 14–15)
- Poster board or card stock
- Glue
- Clear contact paper
- Crayons or markers (optional)
- Scissors
- Storage container for the dominoes (large envelope, berry basket, shoe box, etc.)

What to Do

1. Glue the Animal Dominoes to the poster board. Let dry.

2. If desired, color the animals. Make sure that you color each type of animal the same. For example, color all the horses brown, all the fish blue, and so on.

3. Cover both sides with the clear contact paper.

4. Cut out the dominoes along the heavy lines. Put in the storage container.

5. Put the dominoes with the other manipulatives in your classroom. Follow your standard classroom practice when introducing this activity.

6. As the children play with these cards, show them how to match the animals.

Teaching Sharing

- Encourage the children to take turns matching the animals and to share the cards.

- Comment on all positive behaviors.

- Remind the children that Noah had all of these animals (and more!) on his ark.

They had to share everything, including games and other ways to pass the time.

- Let the children devise their own rules for playing with these cards; they can collaborate in inventing uses for the cards.

Animals with My Feet: An Art Project to Teach the Story

Materials Needed

- Shoes
- Construction paper
- Pencil
- Scissors
- Crayons or markers

What to Do

1. Set up this art project as you would any other assisted art project in your classroom.

2. Help each child place a shoe on the construction paper. Trace around the shoe. This will be the body of the animal.

3. Decide what kind of animal this picture will be. Add legs, head, neck, and so on to the tracing.

4. Let each child color the animal to his heart's delight.

5. Cut out the animal.

Teaching Sharing

- As with the other art projects, help the children enjoy their creations. Devote time to exploring the vividness of the colors, the feeling of the paper, the sound of the scissors, and so on. Focus on the act of creating.

- The animals reveal much about God. As you create this new animal together, talk about how the animals illustrate parts of God: the elephant shows His power, the rabbit shows His gentleness, the bear shows His strength. God has shared His animals with us so we might understand Him better.

- Praise the children for sharing the space at the art table, the art supplies, your attention.

- You might want to display these animals in the classroom instead of sending them home so the whole class can share in the unique beauty of each animal.

Loading the Ark: A Circle-Time Game to Teach Sharing

Materials Needed

- Three small boxes (the arks)
- Three pairs of scissors
- Copies of the Noah's Ark Story Strips (pages 16–18)
- Construction paper, two sheets per team
- Tape (or glue)
- Three teams of children, equal numbers in each team

What to Do

1. Make copies of the Noah's Ark Story Strips. Cut each page into three strips on the solid lines.

2. Divide the class into three teams. Give each team a pair of scissors and three strips from one of the story strip pages. Have each child cut one strip on the dotted line. Encourage the children to share the scissors. (For younger children, you may need to do all of the cutting. If you have more than three children per team, you will have to designate some children "cutters" and some children "deliverers" and maybe some children "assemblers.")

3. Place the small boxes (arks) across the room from the children.

4. Each child will walk to a box and put in his pair of story strip squares. Then he will return to his starting place. Supervise as the children do this. Make sure that each ark has a pair from each story strip page in it.

5. Collect the arks and give one to each team. Help the children correctly assemble the pairs of squares into two correct, complete story strips that illustrate the story of Noah. Show them how to tape the story strips onto the two sheets of construction paper.

Teaching Sharing

- Encourage the children to share the scissors, making sure that they each get a chance to cut some of the story strips. Praise them when they take turns.

- Help them cooperate as they put their pair in the ark. Praise the children as they share the task, the space, and the materials.

- Each team will assemble a pair of story strips, a natural opportunity to reinforce the concept of "pair." To reinforce the concept of "sharing through teamwork," write the names of all the members of the team on each assembled story strip. Display them in your classroom.

Two Tunics Trade: A Circle-Time Game to Teach the Memory Verse

Materials Needed

- Brown paper lunch bags, one per child
- Copies of the tunics (page 19), one tunic per child
- Scissors
- Copy of the Bible memory verse (page 13)

What to Do

1. Make copies of the tunics. Make sure that you have one per child. Cut out the tunics.

2. In half of the bags, put two tunics. Leave the other bags empty. Fold the tops of the bags down.

3. During Circle Time, give each child a lunch bag, keeping one for yourself. Make sure that your bag has two tunics in it. Remind the children to keep the bags closed until it is their turn. Display the Bible memory verse where it can be seen and read.

4. Open your bag. Remove the two tunics and place them in front of you. Help the children repeat the Bible memory verse, referring to the paper.

5. Call on a child and direct her to open her bag. If her bag has two tunics, guide her to put them in front of herself as the class again repeats the memory verse. If her bag is empty, offer to share one of your tunics with her. As she gets the tunic, have the class repeat the Bible memory verse.

6. Repeat this process until every child in the class has one tunic.

7. Plan to repeat this game often during this unit.

Teaching Sharing

- This is a concrete way to "live out" the Bible memory verse. You might need to initially encourage the children with two tunics to offer to share with their "naked neighbors," but the offerings will become spontaneous as the game proceeds.

- Seek similar opportunities to encourage sharing as the children play. For example, when one child has two toys and her friend has none, quote the Bible verse, substituting the toy's name for "tunic." For example, "The girl with two trucks should share with her friend."

Making Tunics to Share: An Art Project to Teach the Bible Memory Verse

Materials Needed

- Large brown paper grocery bags, two per child
- Scissors
- Crayons or markers
- Copy of the Bible memory verse (page 13)

What to Do

1. Cut out a simple tunic from each brown paper bag. (See diagram.)

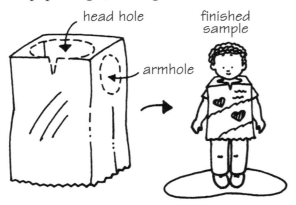

head hole

finished sample

armhole

2. Set up this art project as you would any other independent art project in your classroom.

3. Let each child color the tunic to his heart's delight. Encourage him to make two tunics so he can share one with a sibling, parent, or friend.

4. For those children who can write, encourage them to copy the Bible memory verse onto the tunic.

Teaching Sharing

- As with the other art projects, help the children enjoy their creations. Devote time to exploring the vividness of the colors used, the feeling of the paper, the swish that the tunics make when worn, and so on. Focus on the act of creating.

- Praise the children for sharing the space at the art table, the art supplies, and your attention.

- Ask each child whom she will share her spare tunic with. To reinforce this, you might want to write that person's name inside the tunic. Help each child distinguish between her tunic and the one she will share.

Telling the Story

To tell this story, use toys available in your classroom. Use a set of interlocking blocks to build the ark; gather up your doll-house people to act as Noah and his family; round up various animals to load on the ark. Add a toy bird, people and animal "food," an "olive branch," and a rainbow to your collection. Before telling the story to your class, hand out the props to the children. Give some children the blocks, give others the dolls or animals. Put the "olive branch" where the dove can easily reach it. Read the story (bold print) and follow the instructions (italic print).

Noah and his family were good. They listened to God and obeyed His Word. They lived in a time when most people had forgotten about God; most people did bad things. This made God very unhappy so He decided to destroy the earth and all the people on it.

Then God remembered Noah and his family. God remembered how Noah and his family trusted and obeyed Him. God decided to save Noah and his family. God said, "Noah, there is going to be a great flood. You must build a great big boat

called an ark. Take your family and two of every kind of animal into the boat." Noah listened as God shared His plans. Then Noah obeyed God.

Noah set to work building the ark. *Have the children hand you the blocks.* It was too big for him to build all by himself. He asked his three sons to help him build the ark. *Have them help you build the ark.* The four men shared the work, taking turns with the tools and helping one another. Noah's wife and his sons' wives also worked together collecting the food for the long voyage.

When the ark was finished, the whole family loaded all the animals. They took two of every kind of animal, a mother and a father, into the ark. *Encourage each child to put the animals carefully in the ark. Then have those with dolls put them in the ark while you load some "food."* When all the animals, all the food, and all the people were in the ark, God shut the door. *Shut the door to the ark.*

It began to rain. *Have the children snap their fingers.* It rained and it rained and it rained some more. *Begin to clap your hands softly. Encourage the children to copy you.* For forty days and nights, it rained. *Slap your legs and encourage the children to do the same.* Outside, the water covered everything while inside the ark, it was safe and dry. The animals and Noah's family had to share the space inside the ark. They had to share the food and the drinking water. All the people and all the animals had to try to get along with one another. Noah shared many things.

Finally, God made the rain stop. *Stop slapping, clapping, and snapping.* Noah sent out a bird to find dry land. The dove found an olive branch and gave it to Noah, sharing the good news that the water was going down. *Lift the dove out of the ark and show how it flew with the olive branch.* At last, Noah, his family, and all the animals could go out of the ark. *Help the children unload the ark.* Then God made a beautiful rainbow across the sky. *Hold up the rainbow for your class to see.* God used the rainbow to share His promise that He would never send a flood to destroy the earth again. Noah and his family also made a promise: They promised to be God's people.

Bible Memory Verse

The man with two tunics should share with him who has none.

Luke 3:11 (NIV)

Animal Dominoes

Animal Dominoes

Noah's Ark Story Strips

Noah's Ark Story Strips

Noah's Ark Story Strips

Two Tunic Trade

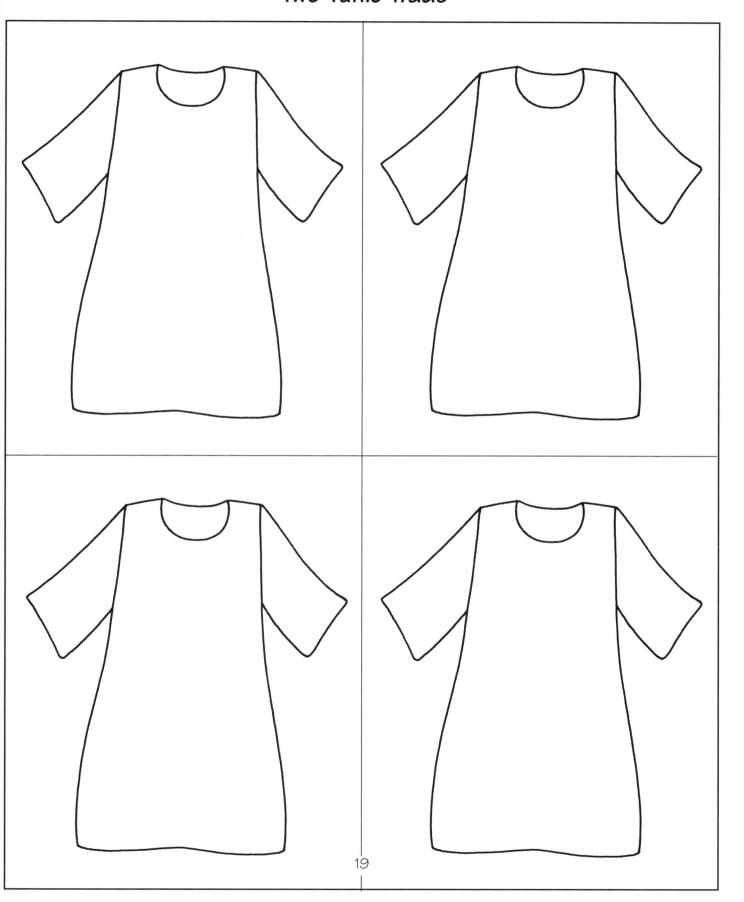

Dear Parent(s),

"Please share!" How many times each day do you say these words to your child? All children must learn to share. This month, our class will learn about Noah and the ark and how Noah's family shared their faith and the task of building the ark with each other, and their temporary home with all the animals. To help teach the story of Noah's ark and the concept of sharing, we will be building an ark for our classroom. On _____ please send one of your child's toy animals to school (not the absolute "can't sleep without" favorite); we'll be using them in our classroom ark for a while. Please label the animal with your child's full name.

The lessons of Noah and sharing shouldn't stop at the classroom door. I invite you to share these lessons with your child at home by reading the story of Noah from a preschool Bible, trying the activities provided in this letter, and teaching this Bible memory verse.

The man with two tunics should share with him who has none. *Luke 3:11*

Learning to share takes time and practice. You can help your child learn to share by first knowing how children share at different ages.

How Children Learn to Share

Age 3: Your 3-year-old has started to imitate sharing behavior, but she still sees herself as the center of the world and is unable to fully understand how her actions affect others. Your child might understand that she is angry when another child will not share a toy, but she is only beginning to understand how the other child might feel when he doesn't get a turn with the toy. At 3, your child can practice asking permission to play with a toy and practice taking turns. You can show your child how to share by willingly sharing your time and possessions with her and others. Use words to point out how you are sharing, for example, "Daddy likes apple pie. I'll share half of my pie with him." "I'd like to share my time with you; let's read a story together." "Let's share the play dough; I'll take half and you can have half."

Age 4: Your 4-year-old is beginning to understand *why* it is important to take turns and share. He begins to want playmates with whom he can share, take turns, fight, and cooperate. Parallel play (playing next to each other in the same space but playing independently) is replaced by interactive play (play that requires sharing). You can encourage, demonstrate, and reinforce sharing and cooperation so your child's attempts at interactive play and friendships are successful.

Age 5: Your 5-year-old shows a great desire to cooperate. She wants to be good and please you. She can play with one or two other 5-year-olds, sharing materials, taking turns, and cooperating to work toward a shared goal. Now you can help move your child toward a more sophisticated form of sharing—shared responsibility. "Chore Charts" can help a child understand her role in the shared responsibilities of the family and "turn-taking" can be shared by siblings.

Sharing isn't just a challenge for children, it's a struggle for parents too. As you struggle daily to share your time, talents, and faith, and encourage your child to share, turn to your heavenly Father in prayer.

Parent's Prayer

Heavenly Father, You taught Noah's family to share their faith and the task of building the ark with each other, and their temporary home with all the animals. So also teach me to share my time and talents with my child. Help me remember that my child will learn best from my example. When I willingly share my faith, time, tools, favorite snack, smile, and kind words with my child, he will learn to share too. In Jesus' name I pray. Amen.

Together in Christ,

Family Activities

Animal Cookies to Share: A Cooking Adventure

Ingredients

½ cup butter or margarine

3 cups quick-cook oatmeal

1 cup honey

3 tablespoons cocoa powder

¾ cup powdered milk

½ teaspoon salt

2 teaspoons vanilla

½ cup peanut butter

½ cup raisins

What to Do

1. Put the butter in a large microwavable dish. Microwave until melted.

2. Stir in the oatmeal until well mixed.

3. Add the remaining ingredients. Mix well with your hands. The dough will be stiff.

4. Wash your hands. Place a bowl of water on the work surface. Wet your hands before shaping the dough into little fish or snakes or any other animal shape.

5. Now you can either:
   a.) Put shapes on a greased cookie sheet. Bake for 10 to 12 minutes at 350°.

   Or

   b.) Put shapes on an ungreased cookie sheet. Refrigerate for 30 minutes.

Teaching Sharing

- Cooking together requires teamwork and cooperation. The chefs must share the measuring cups, the bowls, the ingredients, the recipe, and the work space. Comment on the sharing that spontaneously occurs while making these cookies.

- As you shape the cookies into simple animals, deliberately form them into pairs. Link the pairs of cookies to the story of Noah's ark. Ask your child to tell you the story. Prompt him or her if necessary. Be sure to emphasize the sharing that must have occurred on the ark.

- The finished cookies also beg to be shared. Will you share them with the family? Will you share them with some neighbors? Will you share them with the church? How will you share these cookies?

Making Noah's Ark: A Quiet-Time Activity

Materials Needed

- Milk carton (quart size works best)
- Scissors or utility knife

What to Do

1. Cut the milk carton in half lengthwise. Wash and dry the inside.
2. Let dry completely before using for water or land play.

Teaching Sharing

- This project requires that you share your time with your child. Help him or her to understand that Noah shared his time and energy when he built the real ark.

- Since this project yields two arks, you have a built-in opportunity to share one with a sibling or a friend.

- You might want to use this ark to play out the story of Noah's ark by loading it with plastic animals and dolls. Talk about how crowded the ark is and how the animals had to divide up the space, food, and Noah's attention.

How Things Are Built: Taking a Trip

Materials Needed

- A building site

What to Do

1. Take a trip to a building site. Stop and look at what is going on. Talk about what you see. Help your child to develop his or her "construction-related" vocabulary.

2. If the construction workers are present, point out any cooperation of effort and sharing of tools that you notice.

Teaching Sharing

- Children thrive on repetition. As with the at-home projects described above, use this trip as an opportunity to discuss the story of Noah's ark again. Talk about all the things Noah shared during the building process: his tools, his building plans, the Word of God, and so forth. He had to divide the tasks among his family and they all had to join forces or the ark could not have been completed.

- Talk about the sharing that will go on in this building once it is completed. If it will be a house, mention that a family will create a shared environment within its walls. If it will be a store, talk about all the merchandise that can be bought and shared.

Easy Stuff

1. Buy animal crackers for a special snack. Use the crackers to tell the story of Noah.

2. Use your child's stuffed and toy animals as a focus for playtime and bath time to repeat the story of Noah. You can also explore colors (the rainbow), the number 2, water, things that float or sink, rain and weather, and promises (God kept His promise).

3. Use bath time to illustrate the concept of "flood." Set a few plastic animals and a boat on "dry land" (the bottom of the tub). Then send the "rain" (shower or faucet) and watch the flood wash away the animals and make the boat float.

Follow Directions!

Jonah Learns to Obey

Bible Memory Verse

We will listen and obey.
Deuteronomy 5:27

Teacher's Prayer

Heavenly Father, You taught Jonah to listen to You and to follow Your instructions. So also help me to hear Your Word and do Your will. Father, help me listen to the children in my care the way You listen to me—with Your full attention, patience, love, and faithful response—that I might teach by Your perfect example. In Jesus' name I pray. Amen.

Teaching Objective: Obedience

To help children learn to listen, follow directions, and obey rules, just as Jonah learned to listen to and obey God.

Through God's Word and the power of the Holy Spirit, by the end of this unit, the children should be able to:

1. Tell the basic story of Jonah.

2. Repeat the Bible memory verse.

3. Comprehend the teaching objective *obedience.*

4. Show an increased ability to follow directions.

5. Tell a friend something about God, just as Jonah did.

Learning to follow directions takes time and practice. To follow instructions, a child must listen, understand words, and have the desire to do what is asked. You can help the children learn to follow directions by first recognizing and remembering how children follow directions at different ages and developmental stages.

How Preschoolers Learn to Follow Directions

Age 3: A 3-year-old learns by repetition. He is not always able to remember instructions or rules from one minute or situation to the next so you will have to repeat the same instructions over and over again. He is easily distracted and needs help to focus on your voice and words. To help him obey, you will need his full attention. You can use the words, "I need your eyes and ears," even gently holding his face and looking into his eyes. When you have his attention, give your instructions slowly and clearly giving no more than three instructions at a time. Ask the child to repeat what you told him—"What did my words say?" You can help the children learn to listen by modeling good listening behavior—when children talk to you, give them your full attention, make eye contact, repeat the words they use, and respond to their requests whenever possible.

Age 4: 4-year-olds are often *able* to follow directions but lack the *desire* to conform. They may be argumentative as they struggle with their newfound independence and sense of control of their environment. Their ability to use language shows itself in fewer physical temper tantrums but in an increase in negative words and responses. You can increase a 4-year-old's success in following directions if you give her some time to process your request and then more time to take action. 4-year-olds also have difficulty retaining information because they are so interested in everything around them. Their brains are literally "cluttered" with bits of information, and it's often hard to focus on the present demand. Humor can work wonders when trying to get a resistant 4-year-old to follow directions.

Age 5: 5-year-olds tend to be obedient; they want to "follow the rules" and make others happy. They are able to understand your instructions, retain information, and take action as directed. The children will be more consistent in following classroom and family rules. A 5-year-old is more likely to be interested in listening to instructions and following directions because he now takes pride in a completed project, not just in the process of creating as he did at younger ages.

Teaching Activities

Decorate the Bible Memory Verse: Fish and Fun

Materials Needed

- Copies of the Bible memory verse (page 31), one per child
- Blue and/or green watercolor paints
- Paintbrushes, various sizes
- Fish shapes, 2 or 3 fish per child
- Crayons or markers
- Glue
- Small bowls to hold glue
- Glue brushes or cotton swabs

What to Do

1. The first part of this project is to paint the Bible memory verse. Before school starts, set up for the watercolor part of this art project as you normally set up a painting project. Put the watercolor paints and the paintbrushes on the work table.

2. Show the children how to paint the entire Bible memory verse page blue, green, or some combination of the col-

ors. Label the Bible memory verse with the child's name. Set it aside to dry.

3. The second part of this project is to add the fish shapes. Before school starts, set up for the coloring and gluing part of this art project as you normally do. Put the fish shapes, crayons or markers, and small bowls of glue on the work table.

4. Show the children how to decorate the fish by coloring them. Then help them glue the completed fish on the Bible memory verse.

Teaching Obedience

- To provide practice in following directions, this project has several steps. Be sure to explain each direction clearly. When the children follow the directions, praise them for being obedient.

- Read the Bible memory verse to each child. Talk about how important it is to listen so we are able to obey. Help the children list times that they were able to successfully follow directions.

- Remind the children to share the materials, just as Noah shared with the animals in our unit last month.

- Remind them that sharing is a classroom rule that they must follow.

Keeping the Teaching Objective Alive in the Classroom: Catching Jonah's Fish

Materials Needed

- Styrofoam meat trays, washed
- Scissors
- Copy of Jonah's Fish Procedure Cards (page 33)
- Cardboard
- Glue
- Laminate or clear contact paper

- Hole punch
- Yarn
- A water and sand play table
- A small box
- **Week 1:** Water and small fishing net
- **Week 2:** Rice and funnel
- **Week 3:** Paper scraps and tongs
- **Week 4:** Cornmeal and slotted spoon

What to Do

1. Cut 10–12 fish from the Styrofoam meat trays. Each fish should be about the size of a playing card. Place in the small box.

2. Cut apart the Jonah's Fish Procedure Cards. Glue to the cardboard and then laminate or cover with clear contact paper. Use the hole punch and the yarn to make the cards into a book.

3. Fill the water and sand table with the appropriate material: water, rice, paper scraps, or cornmeal.

4. Put the appropriate utensil in the small box with the fish.

5. Set up the water and sand play table as you normally would. Put the small box with the fish and the utensil, as well as the Procedure Cards, on top of or beside the play table.

6. When introducing this new center to the children, explain that they must follow the Procedure Cards to set up, play with, and put away this activity.

Teaching Obedience

- This whole activity is full of opportunities for the children to follow directions. Praise them when they carefully follow the Procedure Cards. Point out that these cards are directions.

- Remind them of the rules that govern play at the table: no splashing, no throwing the paper/rice/cornmeal, no eating the fish, and so on. Applaud their obedience.

- Are the children sharing the materials? If so, give them a hearty "Good job!" If not, gently urge them to remember Noah and to follow his example. This is also a way that they can follow directions.

God Said to Jonah: A Circle-Time Game to Teach Obedience

Materials Needed

- None

What to Do

1. This game is a variation of "Simon Says," using the phrase "Jonah Says." Try to have some of your directions echo the story: "Swim like a fish." "Run away from God." "Preach the Word." and so on.

2. In Circle Time, explain the rules to your class. You may choose to play elimination style or simply allow all the children to continue playing.

Teaching Obedience

- Praise the children for following your directions correctly. Give extra praise if they recognize the presence or absence of "Jonah says."

- Explain that it's important to listen carefully to words so they can follow directions. The hardest part of listening is not necessarily hearing the words, but remembering them and following through.

- Try incorporating this game into class transitions: moving to the snack table, lining up, choosing books to read.

"Teacher says, if you have blue shoes, line up. Way to follow directions, Lauren and Jimmy." "Red shoes, line up! Andrew, I didn't say 'Teacher Says.' "

Glitter Fish: An Art Project to Teach the Story

Materials Needed

- Light-colored construction paper, 3 or 4 pieces
- Dark-colored marker
- Waxed paper, one sheet per child
- Masking tape
- Yarn
- Scissors
- Glue
- Small flat dish
- Glitter

What to Do

1. Set up for this art project as you normally would.

2. Use the dark marker to draw a simple fish symbol on the construction paper. The traditional Christian symbol works very well in this project. Tape the construction paper to the work surface.

3. Cut the yarn into lengths just long enough to outline the fish symbol. Cut one piece of yarn per child.

4. Pour the glue into the small flat dish. You may want to mix it with a little water.

5. Place a sheet of waxed paper over the drawing. Tape it securely in place.

6. Show the children how to dip a piece of yarn in the glue and use it to outline the fish design. Use one piece of waxed paper for each child.

7. Sprinkle with glitter.

8. Let the fish dry overnight on the waxed paper.

9. Peel the dried fish from the waxed paper and use another loop of yarn for hanging.

Teaching Obedience

- As you help the children make their fish, review the story of Jonah and the big fish. Remind them that Jonah was in the fish for three whole days and nights.

- Praise the children for following directions, regardless of how imperfect their finished fish looks. The goal here is the process of following directions. The finished product is secondary.

- Are the children sharing the materials? If so, give them a hearty "Good job!" If not, gently urge them to remember Noah and to follow his example. This is also a way that they can follow directions.

Walking to Nineveh: An Action Activity to Teach Obedience

Materials Needed

- 10 or 12 pieces of newspaper, folded in quarters
- Masking tape

What to Do

1. Lay out a winding path using the folded newspapers as stepping stones. Use fewer pieces for younger children, more for older ones.

2. Tape the newspaper to the floor to keep it from sliding.

3. Have the children walk on the path.

4. Ask them to skip, hop, jump, crawl, march, and so forth on the path.

Teaching Obedience

- Use this activity to build up the children's activity and movement vocabulary. Help them learn what hop, jump, crawl, etc. mean.

- Applaud the children as they follow your directions and move along the path. Remind them how much easier it would have been for Jonah if he had followed God's directions.

- Children who are waiting for their turn are also following directions: sitting still, being quiet, and listening. Honor their efforts also.

Patterns for Jonah: A Manipulative to Teach Obedience

Materials Needed

- Pretzel sticks or toothpicks
- Play dough
- Fruit loop cereal

What to Do

1. Stick several pretzel sticks into the small chunks of play dough.

2. Fill up each stick with a different pattern of fruit loop cereals (for example, red-blue-red-blue-red).

3. Arrange a corresponding number of empty pretzel sticks and provide the materials for the children to copy your patterns.

Teaching Obedience

- Children must follow your directions, this time using fine motor skills, to successfully complete the activity. You can repeat many of the encouraging suggestions written above. Preschoolers thrive on repetition.

- The hardest part of this activity may be for the children *not* to eat the materials. Praise them for their restraint. For those that nibble, gently remind them to follow your directions and refrain from eating the supplies.

Drip, Drop, Down: A Game to Teach the Bible Memory Verse

Materials Needed

- Clothespins, 2 or 3 per child
- Coffee can or other large-mouthed container
- Copies of the Human Shapes (page 32), enough to place one person on each clothespin
- Large fish shapes, enough to cover the coffee can
- Crayons (optional)
- Scissors
- Masking tape
- Copy of the Bible memory verse

What to Do

1. Cut out the human shapes and the large fish shapes. Color them, if desired.

2. Tape the human shapes onto the clothespins. Tape the large fish shapes on the coffee can so it seems that the can's opening is the fish's mouth. (See diagram.)

clothespin with human shape

coffee can with large fish

3. During Circle Time, give each child 2 or 3 clothespins. Show them how to drop the pins (Jonah) into the coffee can (the big fish).

4. Help them recite the Bible memory verse as they drop Jonah into the fish.

Teaching Obedience

- Pairing speaking with action produces powerful learning. Here the children recite the Bible memory verse as they act out the story. It can produce an awesome understanding of the lesson of the story: follow God's directions.

- Praise the children for their obedience, both while playing the game and while waiting their turn. Following directions can be active or passive—this game is both.

- Jonah was sent to share God's Word. When the children repeat the Bible memory verse, they are also sharing God's Word. This too is a way to be obedient to God.

Simply Put Puzzles: A Manipulative to Teach the Bible Memory Verse

Materials Needed

- Copies of the Simply Put Puzzles (pages 34–39)
- Cardboard
- Glue
- Clear contact paper
- Scissors
- Self-sealing plastic bags
- Small basket

What to Do

1. Make a single copy of each of the Simply Put Puzzles.
2. Glue each puzzle to a separate piece of cardboard and let dry.
3. Cover the puzzles with clear contact paper.
4. Cut the puzzles out along the solid black lines. Put each puzzle in a separate self-sealing plastic bag. Put the bags in the basket.
5. Introduce this new center as you normally would. Encourage the children to put the puzzles away when they have completed them.

Teaching Obedience

- Whenever possible, read the Bible memory verse on each puzzle aloud with the child. Ask him how he can "listen and obey" in the classroom or at home.

- Point out to the child how the puzzles show other children listening and obeying.

- Ask the children, "Are the puzzle kids following directions? Tell me about the pictures."

- Puzzles easily reinforce the concept of following directions. If the children follow directions, they will successfully complete the puzzle. If not, the picture won't be completed. You might need to help the children understand this.

- Praise the children for putting the puzzles away. This is the final instruction for them to follow.

Telling the Story

To tell the story this month, act out the story as you tell it. Encourage the children to follow your lead and to pantomime the story with you. Directions for action are written in italics; all you have to do is follow them.

This is the true story of a man named Jonah. We know it is true because it is in the Bible. Everything written in the Bible is true; none of its stories are make-believe. Even though this is a pretty amazing story, scholars (that's people who study the Bible) know that this is a true story. As I tell the story, copy my actions.

Begin with the children sitting at your feet. One day, the Lord said to Jonah, "Go to the great city of Nineveh and preach against it. It is a city full of bad people who do really bad things. I will destroy it."

Jonah was scared. *Make a scared face.* He decided not to follow directions, and he ran away. *Run in place.* He ran down to the Great Sea and got onto a ship sailing far away. *Pretend to get on the ship. Sway back and forth gently.*

While the ship was sailing, the Lord sent a big storm to blow the ship about. *Move about wildly, as if the storm were tossing you around.* The sailors were very scared. *Make a scared face again.* They cried out to pretend gods to save them. *Hold your hands up as if imploring the gods to answer you.* They threw things into the water. *Pantomime throwing things over the side.* Nothing helped. It looked like the ship was going to sink.

Where was Jonah? He was asleep! *Lay your head on your hands. Close your eyes.* The captain woke him up—*open your eyes and lift your head*—and said, "Jonah! How can you sleep in this storm? Ask your God to make it stop!"

Jonah answered, "I worship the one true Lord, who made the sea and the land. I am running away from Him. He told me to go to Nineveh, but I didn't follow directions."

The sailors asked him, "What should we do to make the sea calm down?" Jonah answered, "Pick me up and throw me into the sea. Then the storm will stop. I know

it is my fault that this great storm is here." The sailors picked up Jonah and threw him into the sea; *they* knew how to follow directions! *Pretend to lift Jonah and throw him overboard.* As soon as Jonah hit the water, the Lord stopped the storm. The ship sailed safely home. *Wipe your brow with relief.*

But what happened to Jonah? Well, the Lord sent a great big fish (some people think it might have been a whale) to swallow Jonah. *Crouch down really small.* For three days and three nights, Jonah was inside the big fish. While he was in the fish, Jonah prayed to God. *Get on your knees and pray.* He promised to obey the Lord and go to Nineveh.

When Jonah got to Nineveh, he began to preach. *Walk slowly.* For three days, he walked the streets and said, "The Lord will destroy Nineveh in 40 days. The Lord will destroy Nineveh in 40 days." When the king heard this, he put on a robe made out of goat's hair and dumped dirt all over himself. *Pantomime dressing yourself. Sit on the floor. Dump a bucket over your head.* He told all his people to pray to the Lord and to stop doing bad things. All the people obeyed the king. *Fold your hands in prayer.* The Lord saw that the people were very sorry and that they were trying hard to do good things. He decided not to destroy the town.

Because Jonah obeyed the Lord, the king and the whole town of Nineveh were saved.

Bible Memory Verse

We will listen and obey.

Deuteronomy 5:27 (NIV)

Human Shapes

Jonah's Fish Procedure Cards

Simply Put Puzzles

We will listen and obey.
Deuteronomy 5:27

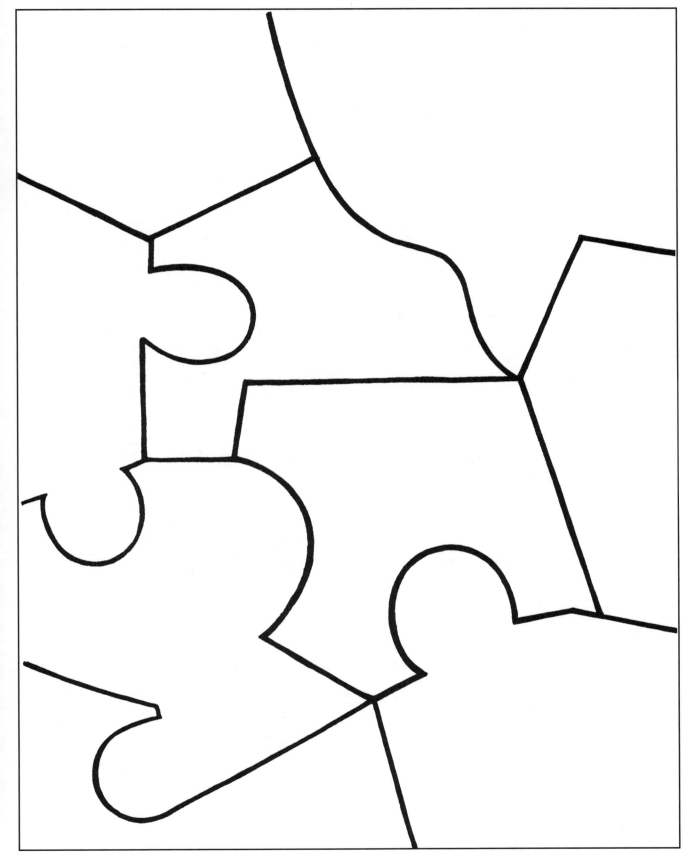

Simply Put Puzzles

We will listen and obey.
Deuteronomy 5:27

Simply Put Puzzles

We will listen and obey.
Deuteronomy 5:27

Dear Parent(s),

"Please follow directions!" "Please do what I tell you to do." You probably repeat these words many times to your child every day. Young children must learn to listen and follow directions so they can be safe, have fun, and learn.

This month, our class will learn about Jonah and his struggle to listen to God and follow His instructions. We will also emphasize the importance of listening to teachers, parents, and friends. The lessons of Jonah and obedience shouldn't stop at the classroom door. I invite you to share these lessons with your child at home by reading the story of Jonah from a preschool Bible, trying the activities provided in this letter, and teaching this Bible memory verse.

We will listen and obey. *Deuteronomy 5:27*

Learning to follow directions takes time and practice. You can help your child learn to follow directions by first understanding how children follow directions at different ages.

How Children Learn to Follow Directions

Age 3: Your 3-year-old learns through repetition. As frustrating as it may be to repeat the same instructions over and over again, this is how your 3-year-old must learn. She cannot always remember instructions or rules from one minute or situation to the next. She is easily distracted and must be helped to focus on your voice and words. To get her full attention, it helps to say, "I need your eyes and ears" while gently holding her face and looking into her eyes. When you have her attention, give your instructions slowly and clearly with no more than three instructions at a time. Ask your child to try to repeat what you told her. You can also help your child learn to listen by modeling good listening behavior—when she talks to you, give her your full attention, repeat the words she uses, and follow her instructions whenever possible.

Age 4: 4-year-olds are often *able* to follow directions but may lack the *desire* to obey. They may be more argumentative as they struggle with their newfound independence and sense of control over their environment. Their ability to use language shows itself in fewer physical temper tantrums but in increased negative words and responses. You can increase your 4-year-old's success in following directions if you give him time to process your request and then more time to take action. 4-year-olds also have difficulty retaining information because they are so interested in everything around them. Their brains are literally "cluttered" with bits of information and it's often hard to focus on the present demand. Humor can work wonders when trying to get a resistant 4-year-old to follow directions.

Age 5: 5-year-olds tend to be obedient; they want to "follow the rules" and make others happy. They are able to understand your instructions, retain information, and take action as directed. She will be more consistent in following family and classroom rules. Your 5-year-old is more likely to be interested in listening to instructions and following directions because she now takes pride in a completed project, not just in the process of creating as she did at younger ages.

Following directions isn't just challenging for children, it's a struggle for parents too. As you struggle daily to obey God's Word, live a God-pleasing life, and lead your child toward obedience, turn to your heavenly Father in prayer.

Parent's Prayer

Heavenly Father, You taught Jonah to listen to You and to follow Your instructions. So also help me to hear Your Word and do Your will. Father, help me to listen to my child the way You listen to me—with Your full attention, patience, love, and faithful response—that I might teach by Your perfect example. In Jesus' name I pray. Amen.

Together in Christ,

Family Activities

Seaside Snack: A Cooking Adventure

Ingredients

Fish-shaped crackers

Pretzel sticks

Chocolate candies

Peanuts

Oyster crackers

Parmesan cheese

Materials Needed

- Wooden spoon
- Large mixing bowl
- Individual serving dishes
- Miniature paper umbrellas (optional)

What to Do

1. Pour "enough" fish crackers (fish), peanuts (rocks), pretzel sticks (fishing poles), oyster crackers (seashells), and chocolate candies (sunken treasure) into the large bowl. Stir with the wooden spoon.

2. Sprinkle Parmesan cheese (sand) on top. Spoon into individual serving dishes and top with an umbrella.

3. Enjoy!

Teaching Obedience

- God created fish and He created the water to be their home. Remind your child that God created the water and that the fish follow His directions and live there.

- When making this snack, be sure to read the directions aloud. Emphasize that you are following directions. You might even want to expand the directions and instruct your child to add the ingredients one at a time. As you enjoy your snack together, talk about the benefits of obedience—in this case, a tasty treat!

- Help your child recite the Bible memory verse. Are you listening to each other? Are you obeying the basic rules of kitchen safety as well as the directions in the recipe?

- Use this recipe as an opportunity to discuss the story of Jonah. Ask your child to tell you the story; supply details when necessary. Emphasize that, in the end, Jonah followed God's directions.

Stay within the Lines: A Quiet-Time Activity

Materials Needed

- Cornmeal *or* sugar *or* rice *or* sand
- Jelly roll pan

What to Do

1. Assemble all the materials.
2. Pour the cornmeal (or other ingredient) into the jelly roll pan.
3. Show your child how to write with her finger in the cornmeal or other material.
4. Show her how to copy your horizontal and vertical lines. Demonstrate how to connect these lines to make squares and triangles.
5. Try drawing circles and letters.

Teaching Obedience

- Many young children are interested in writing before their fine-motor control is developed sufficiently to allow them to master the use of a pencil. Using this method of "writing" allows your child to struggle with writing rather than with the writing implement.

- Urge your child to follow your directions and copy what you draw. Then reverse roles and you copy him. Praise him for his efforts and his obedience.

- The goal here is following directions; pretty lines and shapes are an added benefit. Focus on the process and not the outcome. Eventually, all children learn to write. Blessed is the child who can also follow directions.

A Family Treasure Hunt: A Move-Around Activity

Materials Needed

- 7 to 10 index cards
- Pen or pencil
- Small treasure (piece of candy, new marker, sticker, penny)

What to Do

1. Write 7 to 10 clues, directing your child to go from room to room or to perform a certain activity. For example: Clue 1 might read "Go to the kitchen. Lay down under your chair. Look up. Do you see the next clue?" Clue 2 is taped to the bottom of the child's chair.

2. Stash your clues in the appropriate places. Place Clue 1 in an obvious place (like your child's breakfast plate or pillow.)

3. Read each clue to your child. Joyfully discover the treasure at the end of the hunt.

Teaching Obedience

- Each clue is a direction that your child must follow. Praise her as she listens to and follows each instruction.

- When Jonah finally followed God's directions, he reaped a wonderful treasure—an obedient heart. When the people of Nineveh heard Jonah's message, they followed God's instructions and repented their evil ways. Their reward was redemption and life.

  Jonah's path to Nineveh was not a direct one. It involved backtracking and running away, a sea voyage, a three-day stay in a big fish, and finally many days of walking. As your child struggles to follow your directions, remind him of Jonah's struggles and ultimate success.

Easy Stuff

1. Go to your church's pulpit where the Word of God is proclaimed. Jonah proclaimed God's Word when walking through the town of Nineveh.

2. Put fish toys in your child's bath. Try to find a human figure small enough to fit inside one of the fish. (If younger siblings are around, make sure that this toy is not small enough to choke on.)

3. Listen to books on tape in the car and at home. Your child must follow directions ("beep") to know when to turn the page.

Use Your Words!

Moses Talks to God

Bible Memory Verse

I will help you speak and will teach you what to do. *Exodus 4:15*

Teacher's Prayer

Heavenly Father, You gave Moses the courage and ability to use his words to express Your instructions and laws. Please guide my words as I teach the children in my care to communicate. Remind me to keep my words simple, encouraging, and kind. Guide my continuing study of Your Word so I can lead the children in my care to understand and love Your Word of Law and Gospel. In Jesus' name I pray. Amen.

Teaching Objective: Communication

To help children learn to use their words to communicate feelings, wants, and information, just as Moses talked to God, Pharaoh, and the Israelites.

Through God's Word and the power of the Holy Spirit, by the end of this unit, the children should be able to:

1. Tell the basic story of Moses and the burning bush.

2. Repeat the Bible memory verse.

3. Comprehend the teaching objective *communication*.

4. Show an increased ability to use words to communicate.

5. Demonstrate pre-writing or basic writing skills.

It takes time, practice, and a significant vocabulary to communicate effectively. You can help the children learn to use their words by first recognizing and remembering how children communicate at different ages.

How Preschoolers Learn to Communicate

Age 3: At 3, a child has many words in her vocabulary but often needs help using these words to express herself. Hitting, name calling, tears, tantrums, grabbing, and yelling are all attempts at self-expression and communication. You can help the 3-year-old identify words that describe what her behavior is expressing. You can say, "You're angry that your friend won't share the truck. No hitting. Tell her with your words." Or "You'd like to use the purple crayon. No grabbing. Use your polite words to ask for it." Starting at 3, it's great to introduce the fine art of negotiation. Encourage and assist children in using words to bargain for what they want.

Age 4: 4-year-olds understand the power of words and sometimes use them to shock or hurt. Although it's disturbing to hear ugly words in the classroom, recognize these expressions as positive steps toward the mastery of language. You can use this opportunity to set rules about hurtful words. Praise a child for using words instead of fists or tantrums, while giving him appropriate words to express feelings, wants, and ideas. Children will also use lots of silly words and rhyming words as they play with language. You can use silly words and humor to defuse anger and gain cooperation. "Amanda, you're keeping all the big trucks for yourself, don't be a figglemiggle."

Age 5: 5-year-olds love to talk. They want to use new and big words, and ask about the meaning of words. They are also interested in written words and will often ask adults to spell words for them or to read words that they see on signs, cereal boxes, billboards, and in books. 5-year-olds enjoy humor and can understand simple jokes. You can encourage the children's love of words by joining in the silly jokes and expressing excitement with each new letter and word discovery. 5-year-olds are generally compliant, so you'll be able to do less reminding and reprimanding; you can concentrate on words of encouragement and praise for directions followed and tasks accomplished.

Teaching Activities

Decorate the Bible Memory Verse: Written Words

Materials Needed

- Copies of the Bible memory verse (pages 51–52), one per child
- Pencils
- Pens

What to Do

1. Two versions of this unit's memory verse have been provided. One has the verse written in dotted lines; the other has solid letters. Children develop fine motor control—and the ability to write—at varying rates. For beginning writers, encourage them to decorate the solid line Bible memory verse with pens and pencils. For more experienced writers, show them how to use either a pen or a pencil to trace the dotted lines of the second Bible memory verse. If you have some children who are already writing well, encourage them to copy the Bible memory verse below the printed letters.

2. Before school starts, set up for this art project as you normally do. Place the

pens and pencils on an accessible table. The memory verse pages should be given to the children individually.

3. Show the children how to write on the appropriate Bible memory verse page.

Teaching Communication

- Read the Bible memory verse to each child. Discuss ways and times that God will help them to speak or use their words. Use examples from the story of Moses and the burning bush.

- Tell the children that Moses is believed to have written the first five books of the Bible. This is another way that Moses "used his words." Because he did this, we have the Bible's words to use today.

- Remind them to share the materials, just as Noah shared. Help them follow directions, as Jonah obeyed God. Encourage them to use their words by writing and solving problems, just as Moses wrote the Pentateuch.

Keeping the Teaching Objective Alive in Your Classroom: A Classroom Post Office

Materials Needed

- Copies of the Message Forms for Post Office (pages 53–54)
- Small boxes, one for each child
- Large box for mailing letters
- Utility knife
- Blue paint
- Stationery
- Envelopes
- Pens, pencils, and other writing implements
- A child's writing desk or other designated writing area
- Mailbag

What to Do

1. Decorate the small boxes as described in the activity on pages 47–8. Make sure that each box is clearly labeled with the child's name. Arrange the mailboxes alphabetically. If you teach more than one class, arrange each class separately.

2. Decorate the larger box to look like a mailbox. Cut a slit in the top for dropping in the mail and a door in the back for taking the mail out.

3. Make copies of the Message Forms for Post Office. Run the copies back to back so they can be folded with the "To" section on the outside and the "Dear" and "Love" sections on the inside.

4. Set up the writing area with stationery, envelopes, and writing implements.

5. Help the children use the writing area to write letters (real or simply scribbled, depending on their abilities) to their classmates. Help them fold the letters and put them in the envelopes. Show them how to write the recipient's name on the front. (You may need to help with this as it must be legible.) Then send them to the mailbox to post their letter. The Parent's Letter encourages parents to send in mail. Let the child put this mail in the mailbox too.

6. Each class day, assign a different person to act as the mail carrier. Help him collect the mail and deliver it to the appropriate mailboxes.

7. Set aside a regular time each day for the children to check their mailboxes and read their mail.

Teaching Communication

- For many young children, writing can be a frustrating task. Help the children express their feelings by labeling them. Do they feel angry? Sad? Frustrated?

- Encourage the children to ask for help with any part of the process. Resist the temptation to respond to only non-verbal clues; instead, help them to communicate their needs verbally.

- When a child successfully completes a letter, label the feelings of triumph. Happy? Proud? Excited?

- Encourage the letter writer to read the letter to its recipient, especially if the letter is written in hieroglyphics or scribbles. Encourage the recipient to say "thank you."

Moses Speaks: A Circle-Time Game to Teach Communication

Materials Needed

- Copies of the "Moses Speaks" Bible Characters (pages 55–56). You will need one character per child and teacher; add more if necessary.

What to Do

1. Seat your class in a circle, making sure that there is an empty space to your left. Show the "Moses Speaks" Bible Characters and help the children name each figure.

2. Give each child a Bible character; make sure that the children know their character's name.

3. Say, "Moses, Moses (or other character's name)." Encourage "Moses" to answer, "Here I am." Then say, "The place at my left side is empty. Come here, Moses." The child holding the Moses card then comes to sit next to you.

4. Continue the game with the child on the right of the newly vacated spot being the caller. Encourage that child to call on a different character. Continue playing until each child has had a chance to be the caller.

Teaching Communication

- The hardest part of listening is not necessarily hearing the words but remembering what has been said. As the children struggle to remember their character names, praise them for paying attention, listening, and answering when called.

- "Moses, Moses!" "Here I am!" This is how the conversation between Moses and God in the burning bush began. Weave the story into the game at every opportunity.

- This game depends on communication for its success. If the children fail to use their words, nothing will happen and the game will be quite dull.

Air Words: An Art Project to Teach Communication

Materials Needed

- 2 or 3 colors of washable tempera paint (bright colors work best)

- Plastic drinking straws, at least one per child

- Water

- 2 or 3 wide deep bowls, one for each color of paint

- Construction paper

- Liquid dishwashing detergent

What to Do

1. Fill each bowl about ⅓ to ½ full of paint. Thin the paint with a little water. Add a few drops of dishwashing detergent. Before school, set up this art project as you normally would. This project will require some adult assistance.

2. Teach the children how to blow out of the straws rather than suck in. Show them how to blow bubbles in the paint until the bubbles fill the bowl and begin to spill over the top (you may need to add more liquid soap if the bubbles are skimpy.)

3. Lay the construction paper over the bubbles. They will pop and leave an interesting design on the paper. Be sure to label the masterpiece with the child's name.

Teaching Communication

- Point out to each child how they must "talk" (or blow) to make the pictures. Hitting the paint just makes a mess.

- Listen very carefully as you lay the paper over the bubbles. Can you hear them popping? Moses had to listen very carefully to all that God said.

Mailboxes: An Art Project to Teach the Story

Materials Needed

- Small boxes, one per child (tissue boxes, cereal boxes, shoe boxes, etc.)

- Art paper

- Glue

- Scissors

- Red, yellow, and orange washable tempera paint

- Three small dishes to hold the paint

- Variety of branches and sticks—if you are really bold, include one or two baby-size sandals

- Marker

What to Do

1. Before the children arrive, cover the boxes with art paper so there is a plain canvas to paint on. Let dry.

2. Pour each color of tempera paint into a separate dish. Set up this project as you would any other art project.

3. Show the children how to paint the boxes using the branches, sticks, and sandals. Let dry.

4. Boldly label each box with the child's name. Assemble (see above) into a post office.

Teaching Communication

- As the children paint, repeat the story to them. Remind them of the various elements of the story represented: branches for the burning bush, sticks for Moses' staff, bright paint for the fire, and sandals for the sandals Moses removed.

- Encourage the children to talk about their masterpieces. Help them discover new words to describe them: bright, bold, scratchy, footprinted, multicolored, etc.

- When more than one child is working on the project, remind them to use their words to get what they want, "Ask for the paint, Andy, use your words." "Caroline, please don't take the brush, ask for it." "Wonderful, Abby, you remembered to say thank you." Remember Noah? Use your words to praise these workers for sharing the supplies and the work space.

Prayer Time: A Center Activity to Teach the Story

Materials Needed

- Child-friendly tape recorder with microphone
- Blank tape

What to Do

1. Set up this activity as you would any new center in your classroom. As the children show interest, teach them how to record their voices. If you created a Moses marching cadence (see "Telling the Rest of the Story"), encourage them to repeat as much of it as they can remember. Help them repeat the Bible memory verse. Help them record prayers they have memorized or made up.

2. Show the children how to play back their recordings. You may want to play the tape back to the entire group during circle time.

Teaching Communication

- Moses had to proclaim the Word of the Lord. As the children speak into the tape recorder, point out that they too are proclaiming the Word of the Lord.

- Moses later recorded his experiences in the book of Exodus. Listen to the children's record of the experiences. Remind them that they have "used their words" to make a memory.

- When more than one child is using the center, encourage them to interview each other.

- Remember Noah? Praise these workers for sharing the supplies and the space. Help them negotiate taking turns, another way of using their words.

Sign Me a Story: A Circle-Time Activity to Teach the Bible Memory Verse

Materials Needed

- Bible Memory Verse Signing Chart (page 57)

What to Do

1. Familiarize yourself with the signs. Practice in front of a mirror. Remember that the illustrations show a right-handed signer. If you are also right-handed, you will need to "reverse" the sign. If you are left-handed, you will need to "mirror" the sign.

2. During Circle Time, repeat the Bible memory verse with the children until they seem comfortable with it. Then teach them the signs. Practice the signs as a class until the children can perform them easily.

Teaching Communication

- Sign language is another form of communication, another way to "use your words."

- Moses had to proclaim the Word of the Lord. As the children make the signs, point out that they too are proclaiming the Word of the Lord.

- God used His Words to give us a promise. He will help us "use our words" even when it seems easier to whine, cry, or hit.

- The hardest part of listening is not necessarily hearing the words, but remembering what has been said. As the children struggle to remember the signs and the Bible memory verse, praise them for paying attention, listening, and participating.

Pinwheel Talk: An Art Project to Teach the Memory Verse

Materials Needed

- Copies of the Pinwheel (page 58), one per child

- Crayons, markers, or other coloring implements

- Child-sized scissors
- Clear tape
- Paper fasteners, one per child
- Plastic straws, one per child

What to Do

1. Set up this project as you would any other art project.

2. Encourage the children to color the pinwheel squares.

3. Help the children cut out the pinwheel squares. Then help them cut along the dotted lines, stopping at the circle. You may need to cut for them.

4. Show the children how to fold the outside corners to the center of the pinwheel. Use small pieces of tape to hold them in place.

5. Push the paper fastener through the center circle of the pinwheel, making sure to catch all four corners.

6. Poke the paper fastener through the plastic straw about one inch from the top.

7. Show the children how to blow their pinwheels to make them spin.

Teaching Communication

- Help the children talk about what they are doing, colors, shapes, line thickness, and crayon speed.

- Label all the feelings the children display: frustration, pride, concentration, joy, amazement, disinterest.

- Point out how you must "talk" (or blow) to make the pinwheel move. Moses also had to talk to Pharaoh to get what he wanted: freedom for God's people.

Telling the Story

Materials Needed

- A burned birthday candle
- A pair of sandals
- A crown
- A strip of brown construction paper
- A white glove
- Some red powdered drink mix
- A pitcher
- A small glass of water

Decorate the brown construction paper to look like a staff on one side and a snake on the other. Hide the white glove inside your shirt. Pour the powdered drink mix into the pitcher. Place the small glass of water by your feet. As you read the story, follow the instructions in italic print.

———————

A long time ago, before you were born, before your parents were born, before even Jesus was born, lived a man named Moses. Moses was an Israelite, which meant that he was part of a people chosen by God. His job was to tend sheep.

One day, as he was tending his father-in-law's sheep, he saw a burning bush. When he looked closely, he realized that the bush did not get burned up by the flames the way a birthday candle does. *Pass around the burned birthday candle.* Moses was afraid but also very curious, and he decided to go closer to see the bush.

Now, the burning bush was really the Lord, who had come down from heaven to talk to Moses. The Lord called to him, "Moses, Moses!" And Moses answered, "Here I am!" Then the Lord said, "Don't come any closer to the bush. You are on holy ground. Take off your sandals!" *Show the children the pair of sandals.* And Moses did just as the Lord told him to do: He

took off his sandals and stood still.

The Lord said, "I am the God of your father. I know the trouble that your people, the Israelites, are having with the Pharaoh in Egypt." (The Pharaoh was the king.) *Put the crown on your head briefly.* The Israelites were his slaves and he was very mean to them. The Lord continued, "I want you to use your words and tell the Pharaoh to let My people leave Egypt."

"But Lord," said Moses. "What if the Pharaoh does not believe me?"

"Then you must do these amazing signs. First, throw your staff onto the ground." Moses obeyed and threw his big stick on the ground. It immediately became a snake. The Lord told Moses to pick it up. When he did, it became a staff again. *Act this out with the strip of brown construction paper.*

"Now," said the Lord, "Put your hand under your shirt, then pull it out." Moses obeyed the Lord again. When he brought his hand out, it was sick and white as snow. *Put your hand into the glove that you have hidden in your shirt. Bring it out with the glove on.* But when he put it back in his shirt and then took it out, it was healed. *Repeat, this time removing the glove.*

For a third sign, the Lord told Moses to pour river water on the ground and it would turn into blood. *Pour the small glass of water into the pitcher with the red powdered drink mix. Show the results to the children.*

Moses was still afraid to talk to the Pharaoh. He said to God, "But, Lord, I am not good at using my words."

The Lord reassured Moses, saying, "I will be with you and teach you what to say. Go, use your words. Talk to the Pharaoh. You talked to Me—you can talk to Pharaoh." And Moses did as God told him to do.

Bible Memory Verse

I will help you speak and will teach you what to do.

Exodus 4:15 (NIV)

Dotted Letter Bible Memory Verse

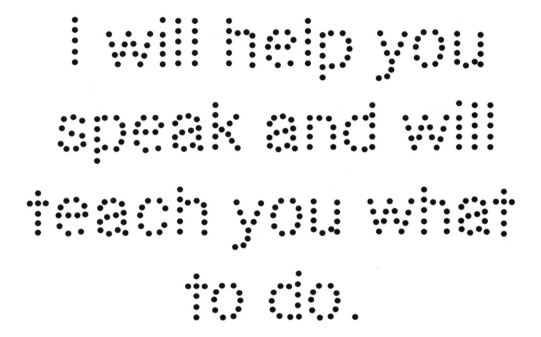

I will help you speak and will teach you what to do.

Exodus 4:15 (NIV)

Message Forms for Post Office (Front)

Dear

fold

Love

Dear

fold

Love

Dear

fold

Love

Dear

fold

Love

Dear

fold

Love

Message Forms for Post Office (Back)

To:

To:

To:

To:

To:

"Moses Speaks" Bible Characters

"Moses Speaks" Bible Characters

Bible Memory Verse Signing Chart

I—index finger points to and touches chest

WILL—flat hand palm facing side of head, arc forward

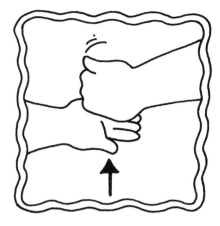

HELP—palm lifts bottom of fist

YOU—index finger points at person

SPEAK—the "4" hand touches chin and moves forward, repeat several times

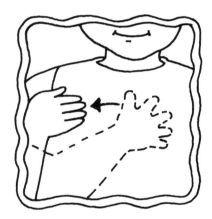

AND—palm faces body "5" hand, pulls to right and draws fingers together

TELL—palm down, index finger touches chin and moves out to become palm up

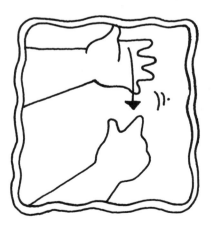

WHAT—index fingertip cuts down left fingers

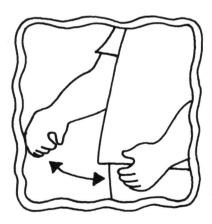

DO—palm down hands in a "C" shape swing slightly back and forth

Pinwheel

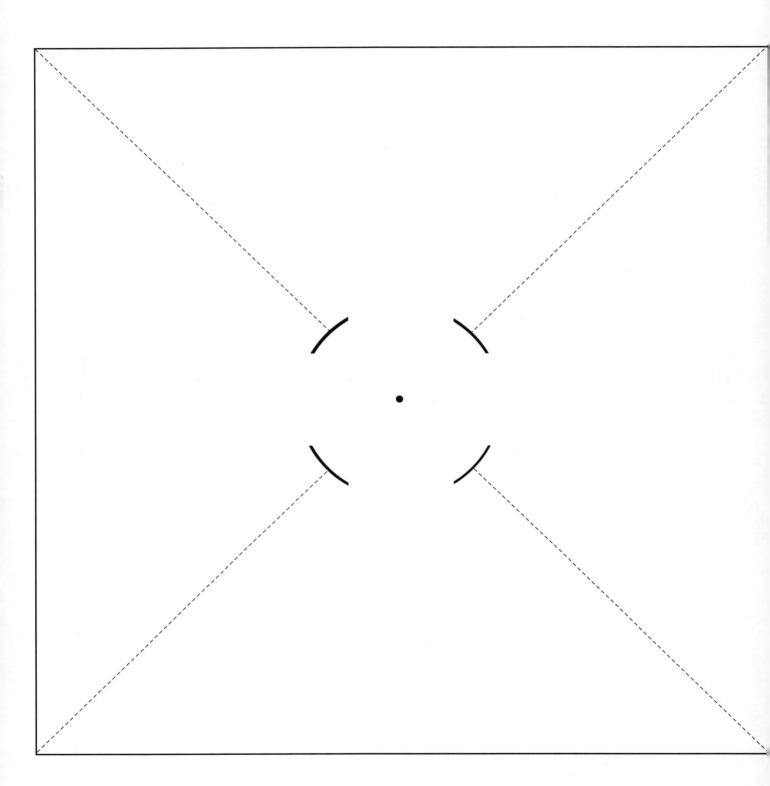

Dear Parent(s),

"Please, use your words." This short phrase, spoken calmly and with encouragement, can help your child begin to connect words with feelings and desires. This month, our class will learn how Moses learned to use his words to speak to and for God. We will emphasize using words to express ourselves and focus on using words to talk to God in prayer. The lessons of Moses and communication shouldn't end in the classroom. I invite you to share these lessons with your child at home by reading the stories of Moses (Moses and the burning bush, Moses speaks to Pharaoh, and the Ten Commandments) from a preschool Bible, trying the activities in this letter, and teaching this Bible memory verse.

I will help you speak and will teach you what to do. *Exodus 4:15*

We will be creating a classroom post office and mailboxes to teach word recognition, sorting, and written communication. You can help fill your child's mailbox by writing short notes on the attached message forms and sending them back to school with your child. You can send as many letters as you want. You might want to print messages like: "I'm thinking of you." "Remember to use your polite words." "Did you play with blocks today?" "I'll be waiting with milk and cookies when you come home." and of course "I love you."

It takes time and practice to communicate effectively. You can help your child learn to use her words by first understanding how children communicate at different ages.

How Preschoolers Learn to Communicate

Age 3: At 3, your child has many words in her vocabulary but often needs help using these words to express herself. Hitting, name calling, tears, tantrums, grabbing, and yelling are all attempts at self-expression and communication. You can help your 3-year-old identify words that describe what her behavior is expressing. You can say, "You're angry that your friend won't share the truck. No hitting. Tell her with your words." Or "You'd like to use the purple crayon. No grabbing. Use your polite words to ask for it." Starting at 3, it's great to introduce the fine art of negotiation. Encourage and help your child use words to bargain for what she wants.

Age 4: 4-year-olds understand the power of words and sometimes use them to shock or hurt. Although it's disturbing to hear ugly words at home, recognize these expressions as positive steps toward the mastery of language. You can use this opportunity to set rules about hurtful words. Praise your child for using words instead of fists or tantrums. Give her appropriate words to express feelings, wants, and ideas. She will also use lots of silly words and rhyming words as she plays with language. You can use silly words and humor to defuse anger and gain cooperation. "Amanda, you're keeping all the big trucks for yourself, don't be a figglemiggle."

Age 5: 5-year-olds love to talk. Your child will want to use new and big words, and ask about the meaning of words. He is also interested in written words and will often ask you to spell words for him or to read words that he sees on signs, cereal boxes, billboards, and in books. 5-year-olds enjoy humor and can understand simple jokes. 5-year-olds are generally compliant, so you'll be able to do less reminding and reprimanding while you concentrate on words of encouragement and praise for directions followed and tasks accomplished.

Communicating isn't a challenge only for children, it's a struggle for parents too. As you work each day to communicate with your child, also remember to use your words to turn to your heavenly Father in prayer. Ask that He guide your thoughts, words, and actions as an example to your child.

Parent's Prayer

Heavenly Father, You gave Moses the courage and ability to use his words to express Your instructions and laws. Please guide my words as I teach my child to communicate. Remind me to keep my words simple, encouraging, and kind. Guide my continuing study of Your Word that I can lead my child to understand and love Your Words of Law and Gospel. In Jesus' name I pray. Amen.

Together in Christ,

Family Activities

Stone Tablet Graham Crackers: A Cooking Adventure

Ingredients
- Graham crackers
- Colored frosting gel in squeeze tubes

What to Do
1. Give your child two graham crackers.
2. Show him how to squeeze the frosting from the tube onto the graham crackers to make letters or designs.
3. Let your child experiment with "writing."
4. Eat the decorated graham cracker snack.

What You Can Talk About
As you begin creating this snack, retell the story, in your own words, of Moses receiving God's words/rules written on two stone tablets.

If your child can print letters or his name, encourage him to use the frosting to write on the crackers. If your child does not yet "write," let him "practice" writing with creative designs.

Ask your child about rules. Ask him to name some rules that he follows at home or school. Remind him of the "use your words" rule.

"Moses Says" Game: A Move-Around Activity

Materials Needed
- "Moses Says" Game Instructions (page 62)

- You
- Your child

What to Do

1. This game is a variation of "Simon Says." As you play this game with your child, use your own words to tell the story of God helping Moses talk to Pharaoh. If you need to refresh your memory on this story, refer to Exodus 5–11.

2. Explain the rules to your child: She is to perform the action described only when it is preceded by the words "Moses Says." If you don't say "Moses Says" first, then tell your child that she is to ignore the direction.

3. Use the instruction sheet as a starting point for giving directions for playing "Moses Says." Make up your own ideas to extend the game.

4. Let your child make up the commands. Encourage other family members to join in as well—but remember that pets don't listen very well.

Teaching Communication

- Point out how powerful words can be. Words can convince people to do things, just as Moses' words convinced Pharaoh to let the Israelites go.

- Explain that it's important to listen carefully to words so your child can follow directions. The hardest part of listening is not necessarily hearing the words, but remembering them and following through on them. Praise your child when he does these steps correctly.

- This is a good opportunity to explain the process of speaking, listening, choosing to follow directions or not, and consequences. Moses told Pharaoh what God wanted him to do, Pharaoh listened and decided not to follow Moses' instructions, God sent bad things to Egypt. Carry this idea into your daily communication with your child: If you tell him to put away his toys and he chooses to disobey, what is his consequence? He loses the privilege of playing with the toy. Young children need to have the process carefully labeled for them, many times, before they begin to catch on.

- This game can also be used to encourage cooperation: "Moses says, put your shoes on." "Moses says, get your book bag." "Do a dance." "Moses says get in the car."

Seeing Words in Print: Taking a Trip

Materials Needed

- Newspaper publishing/printing office
- Telephone

What to Do

1. Call your local newspaper office and ask to arrange a brief tour of the printing plant. At the end of the tour, ask to purchase an "end roll" of newsprint to use for various art projects at home or school.

Teaching Communication

- Point out that you must use polite words when calling to ask for the tour. Explain that it takes courage to ask for something you want. Moses had to have courage to use his words and to ask Pharaoh for freedom. He had to use his words to talk to God in the burning bush—and he was very polite as he talked to God.

- Encourage your child to use his words to ask questions on the tour, and to say "thank you" when the tour is over. Once you are home, help him write a thank-you note to the tour guide (using your written words).

Easy Stuff

1. Identify the number 10, count to 10, count 10 things, recognize numbers 1 through 10. Count 10 things—mailboxes, yellow cars, trees—on your way to school.

2. Talk about rules: God's rules, rules at home, rules at school, rules in public places, rewards for following rules, and consequences for breaking rules. Remind your child that Moses had to follow God's rules and remove his sandals before he could speak to the burning bush.

3. Does the burning bush scare or fascinate your child? Use this as a starting point for discussing fire safety rules and procedures. Discuss your fire escape rules. Remind your child that fire is dangerous.

"Moses Says" Game Instructions

- Moses says, "Wiggle like a flowing river."
- Moses says, "Hop like a frog."
- "Turn around." (Child should not perform this act because Moses did not say it. Remind him to listen for "Moses Says.")
- Moses says, "Buzz like a fly."
- "Blink your eyes."
- Moses says, "Fly like a gnat."
- Moses says, "Bounce like a hailstone.
- "Touch your nose."
- "Stand on one foot."
- Moses says, "Moo like a cow."
- "Clap your hands."
- Moses says, "Neigh like a horse."
- Moses says, "Sneeze like a sick person."
- "Touch your toes."
- Moses says, "Cry like a baby."
- Add more; ask your child for ideas.

Please Help!

Martha Is a Good Helper

Bible Memory Verse

[Help] one another in love. *Galatians 5:13*

Teacher's Prayer

Heavenly Father, in my efforts to be helpful like Martha, I too often get caught up in busy-ness. Martha was very busy preparing for Jesus' visit, trying to do it all, not asking for help until she was overwhelmed, and believing that it was more important to make physical preparations for her Lord than to prepare her heart by listening to His Word. Father, I often need help as I teach the children in my care. Help me remember to prepare my heart as thoroughly as I prepare my lessons. I ask for Your guidance as I plant the seeds of helpfulness in the children in my care. In Jesus' name I pray. Amen.

Teaching Objective: Helpfulness

To help children learn to help others, just like Martha helped get ready for Jesus' visit.

Through God's Word and the power of the Holy Spirit, by the end of this unit, the children should be able to:

1. Tell the basic story of Martha and Mary.
2. Repeat the Bible memory verse.
3. Comprehend the teaching objective *helpfulness*.
4. Show an increased ability to be helpful.
5. Demonstrate use of kitchen utensils.

Encouragement and appreciation go a long way toward developing helpfulness in the children. You can design successful helping tasks and nurture pride in helping others by first understanding and remembering how children are helpful at different ages and developmental stages.

How Children Learn to Help

Age 3: A 3-year-old loves to imitate. He will stand at the chalkboard and help his teacher erase chalk marks. He will follow you around the classroom as you scrub glue off the tables, doing his best with a damp sponge. And he swishes paintbrushes in water at the sink alongside the classroom volunteer. He will help someone who provides companionship and shows him how a task is done. Instead of expecting him to "Put the toys away," you will get better results with, "Please help put the blocks away. I'll pick up the red blocks, you put the blue blocks in the basket." At 3, the children are learning the "how tos" of helping. 3-year-olds must also begin to hear about the rules of helping; they won't usually follow rules on their own, but will imitate someone who is practicing the rules. "After lunch we put the dishes in the sink. Please come and help me with this task."

Age 4: At 4 it is easier to help, cooperate, and share than it was at 3. 4-year-olds are less possessive, understanding that sharing does not mean losing the object forever. At 4, your child has learned many of the steps necessary to complete a task and has the intellectual, emotional, and physical ability to accomplish the task. If you tell her, "Please help, it's your turn to put the dishes in the sink," she's seen you do it, practiced it with your help, and knows the steps required to put dishes in the sink. At 4, she wants to "do it myself" and her definition of "helpful" may sometimes be exasperating to you. To avoid struggles over who is "helping" whom and what is really "helpful," introduce the process of bargaining/negotiating. If she wants to be helpful and prepare the snack herself, expect and accept cracker crumbs on the floor. She can clean it up with the broom and dustpan later, but you can help by pouring milk from the carton into a small pitcher that's easy for her to manage. 4-year-olds are often frustrated when they try to do something "by myself" and can't quite get it right. This is a good time to teach that asking for help is good, just as Martha asked for help from Mary and Jesus.

Age 5: 5-year-olds have a great desire to be helpful, please others, and receive acceptance. A 5-year-old will offer to do something helpful on his own and then report his accomplishment to earn praise and feel proud of himself. This is a great age to introduce Helping Charts with sticker rewards for completing helpful tasks. 5-year-olds follow rules as a way to organize and understand their life and environment. The 5-year-old will be helpful in order to follow an established rule. "At recess, we stand quietly in a straight line, it's the rule." "On Mondays, I empty the wastebaskets, it's the rule." "I make my bed before I eat breakfast, it's the rule." You can praise him for his helpfulness when he follows the rules.

Teaching Activities

Decorate the Bible Memory Verse: Kitchen Utensil Painting

Materials Needed

- Copies of the Bible memory verse (page 70), one per child
- One color of washable tempera paint
- 2 or 3 flat containers to hold the paint
- Assorted kitchen utensils: whisk, slotted spoons, vegetable brush, butter knife, etc.

What to Do

1. Before school starts, set up for this project as you would any painting project.
2. Show the children how to use the various kitchen utensils to paint designs on the Bible memory verse. Encourage them to explore the different patterns each utensil makes, as well as the different ways each utensil can be used.

Teaching Helping

- Read the Bible memory verse to each child. Ask them to list ways that they can help each other in love. Ask for ways that they can help at home.

- Remind the children to share the supplies, just as Noah shared. Encourage them to use their words to settle disputes, just as Moses did. Help them follow directions, just like Jonah did. Explain that these are all ways to help each other in love.

- As with any other art project, the emphasis here should be on the process. Help the children enjoy their work, just as Martha enjoyed hers, by making specific, positive comments on their technique rather than their picture.

Keeping the Teaching Objective Alive in the Classroom: Doing Martha's Work

Materials Needed

- Your usual kitchen corner, plus any of the following:
- Large terra cotta plate (like those found under terra cotta pots) for making bread
- Mortar and pestle (used for grinding wheat to make flour)
- Sieve (used for sifting flour)
- Stoneware or terra cotta dishes (representative of the kind Martha would have used)
- Plastic pitcher

- Laundry basket (optional)
- 5 or 7 small hand towels (optional)
- Bread oven, representative of the one Martha would have used
- Medium-sized cardboard box
- Box cutter
- Brown paint
- Black markers

What to Do

1. Use the box cutter to cut a semicircle in the front of the cardboard box. Cut one small rectangle on each side. (See diagram.) Paint the box brown. Use the black marker to draw bricks on the oven.

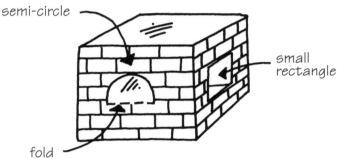

semi-circle

small rectangle

fold

2. Set up your kitchen corner as you normally would. Be sure to include at least some of the food preparation and eating utensils listed above, as these were like the things that Martha would have used as she prepared for Jesus' visit and meal.

3. As they show interest in this activity corner, show the children the bread oven, plate, mortar and pestle, and sieve. Demonstrate how to use them. Explain their role in the story.

4. Tell the children that Martha would have had to carry water from a nearby well. She probably would have carried the pitcher on her head. Encourage the children to try carrying the plastic pitcher on their heads.

5. Up for a challenge? Bring in a laundry basket and some small hand towels. Teach the children how to fold laundry!

Teaching Helping

- The kitchen that Martha used would have been vastly different from the ones that the children are familiar with. With many of the modern conveniences missing, food preparation was an all-day affair for most women. While Martha cooked the food, Jesus had time to teach—that was helpful to Him and His disciples!

- At least 13 unexpected guests had just appeared on Martha's doorstep. She would have to work very hard to prepare their food. She needed all the help that she could get! Imagine, with the children, what the kitchen might have been like when all of the visitors came in to help Martha.

- Encourage the children to share the activity corner (just like Noah) and use their words to settle disputes (just like Moses), and follow directions (just like Jonah). These are all ways to be good helpers.

Clean-up Helpers: A Circle-Time Game to Teach Helping

Materials Needed

- 3 or 5 cotton balls per child
- Drinking straws, one for each child
- Small basket

What to Do

1. During Circle Time, scatter the cotton balls on the floor.

2. Give each child a drinking straw. Demonstrate how to pick up a cotton ball by sucking through the straw. Drop it into the small basket.

3. Encourage the children to help you clean up the Circle Time area by using their straws.

Teaching Helping

- During the game, praise each child by name. Thank him for his help.

- When the area is clean, talk about how Martha cleaned her whole house just for Jesus' visit. Mary probably helped with this, which made it much easier for Martha.

- Remind the children that they can be good helpers at home by cleaning up their toys. Help them understand that their siblings need help cleaning up too, just as Martha needed Mary's help.

Pasta Pictures: An Art Project to Teach the Story

Materials Needed

- Assorted types of cooked pasta (flat pastas like lasagna, fettucine, or spaghetti work best)
- Construction paper (dark colors work best)
- Waxed paper
- Several heavy books

What to Do

1. Before class starts (at home if necessary), cook the pasta until al dente. Be sure to put oil in the cooking water to prevent the pasta from sticking. Keep the pasta moist in plastic bags or sealed plastic containers.

2. Set up for this art project as you normally would. Be sure to be available to help the children move their completed projects to the drying area.

3. Set the drained, cooked pasta in the center of the art table. Place single sheets of construction paper at the work spaces. Show the children how to place the various types of pasta on the construction paper. Explain that they can use the shapes to create an object (such as a house, car, animal, person, etc.) or a design.

4. When each child is finished, cover the picture with a piece of waxed paper. Place several heavy books on the picture and allow it to dry overnight. The starch in the pasta, combined with the weight of the books, should make the pasta stick to the paper.

Teaching Helping

- Remind the children that you did some extra preparation for this craft. Just like Martha, you were a good helper.

- As they listen to your directions, praise them for being good helpers.

- Encourage the children to work together in creating these works of art. They can help each other make wonderful pictures.

Using Martha's Tools: A Manipulative to Teach Helping

Materials Needed

- Scoop, flour, and two suitable containers
- *Or* Wooden spoon, water, and two bowls
- *Or* Funnel, rice, and two suitable containers
- *Or* Ladle, nuts, and two suitable containers
- *Or* Pair of tongs, tea bags, and ice cube trays
- *Or* Mallet, bananas, and resealable bags

What to Do

1. Choose one or more of the kitchen utensils listed above and assemble with other materials. Introduce this activity as you would any other new manipulative. Initially, this activity will require a good deal of supervision. Once several children have mastered the utensils, it

will require less attention. These children can be helpful by teaching others how to use the utensils.

2. Show the children how to correctly use the kitchen utensil. For example, show how to scoop and dump flour or pour rice through the funnel or ladle nuts from bowl to bowl and so on.

Teaching Helping

- Although this activity is time-consuming in the beginning, nurturing these skills has a delightful dividend: a truly helpful kitchen helper!

- Martha was a skilled homemaker. While many of these utensils might have been unfamiliar to her, she could use her own utensils very well.

- Use this activity as an "each one teach one" kind of activity. You teach a few of the children how to use a kitchen utensil, then encourage them to be good helpers and to teach other children. Encourage these other children to teach the remaining children. Choose different children to be the initial teachers with the next utensil—everyone can be a helper!

Making Jesus' Supper: An Activity to Teach Helping

Materials Needed

- Graham crackers, one square for each child
- Peanut butter or cream cheese
- Nuts, raisins, cereal, and other additions
- Plastic knives
- Small plates
- Several small bowls

What to Do

1. Put the nuts, raisins, and cereal into separate bowls. These will be used to decorate the snack.

2. Divide the children into two groups: spreaders and decorators. Show your spreaders how to spread the peanut butter or cream cheese on the graham crackers. To the decorator group, demonstrate how to use the nuts, raisins, and cereal to decorate each snack.

3. Put the snacks on the small plates.

4. Eat!

Teaching Helping

- Remind the children that Martha was busy fixing something for Jesus to eat. The children are also preparing a snack, just like Martha did.

- Praise the children for helping one another prepare the day's snack. Look for examples of the children spontaneously helping one another; lavish praise on these children.

- Are the children sharing the materials? Are they using their words to settle disputes? Are they following your directions? These are all ways to be good helpers. Remind the children that just as Noah, Moses, and Jonah helped God, they too can help you by sharing, talking, and obeying.

Helpful Handoff: A Circle-Time Game to Teach the Bible Memory Verse

Materials Needed

- Small kitchen utensil
- Copy of the Bible memory verse (page 70)

What to Do

- Have the children stand or sit in a circle, holding their palms up. Put a small kitchen utensil on the palm of one child. As the child passes the utensil, help him say the Bible memory verse. Continue around the circle until each child has had a turn.

Teaching Helping

- When we remember God's Word, we are helpers. When you help the children remember the Word, you too are a good helper.

- There are many ways to be helpful: taking turns, saying please and thank you, and picking up after each other. Praise any examples of helping observed during this game.

Good Deed Bread: An Activity to Teach the Bible Memory Verse

Materials Needed

- Large circles cut from brown construction paper, 2 per child
- Dark colored marker
- Ruler
- Scissors
- Tape
- Crayons

What to Do

1. Using the marker and ruler, divide one of each student's construction paper circles into equal pie-slice pieces. Cut along the lines.

2. Write the Bible memory verse on the second circle.

3. Have the children color the Bible memory verse bread to look like the bread that Martha would have served to Jesus.

4. Tape each piece of the first bread onto the Bible memory verse bread.

5. During Circle Time, ask the children to name various classroom tasks (water plants, wash tables, erase blackboard, clean paintbrushes). Be sure that these are tasks performed regularly and that they can be done by the children, either solo or as an assistant. Write each task on a wedge of the first paper bread.

6. Each day, allow children to select a slice of bread and perform the written task. As they select all the tasks, they will see the Bible memory verse revealed underneath on the whole bread. Watch, assist, and praise children as they perform the tasks.

Teaching Helping

- Good deeds are helping deeds. Praise the children for being helpful. Encourage them to do similar helping deeds at home.

- Use this activity to retell the story. What helpful things did Martha do for Jesus? How did Jesus help Martha? How can the children help Jesus?

Telling the Story

Materials Needed

To tell the story in this unit, you will use a flannel board and felt figures. If you have some appropriate felt figures available, feel free to use them. If not, then use the ones found on pages 71–73. Cut them out, pin them to appropriate colored felt and use them as patterns to make your own felt figures. For clothes, either cut the garments from felt or draw them on using fabric paints—markers will work too. Use fine line markers or fabric paint to add details such as facial expressions, fingers, and so on. You can also make these figures out of paper. Put small loops of tape or Velcro brand adhesive on the back to make them stick to the flannel board.

Before You Begin

Before telling the story, place the flannel board where the children can see it. Hand out the felt figures, one to each child. Be sure to identify the figure each child is holding. Tell the children that they will be your helpers and will hand you the figures when you need them.

The story is written in bold print; the directions to follow as you read are in italics.

Some of the stories in the Bible are exciting—like when Moses talked to God in the burning bush. Some of the stories in the Bible are amazing—like when Jonah was swallowed by the big fish. But some of the stories are pretty ordinary, about regular people just like you and me. Even the regular stories are true (everything in the Bible is true), and even ordinary people can teach us a lot about being good followers of Jesus.

Once there were two sisters named Martha and Mary. They were good friends of Jesus, and He often came to visit at their house. *Put up figures of Martha and Mary standing by their house.* One morning, Martha looked out her front door and saw Jesus and His disciples coming toward her house. Martha, wanting to serve Jesus, immediately began to get the house ready for the visit. *Take down the figures of Martha and Mary. Put up the figures of Martha sweeping and cooking.* She swept the floor and cleaned off the chairs. Just as she was about to fix supper for the crowd of people coming to her house, they arrived. She greeted Jesus with a kiss and invited Him to come in. Once inside, Jesus started to teach. Mary sat at Jesus' feet and listened while Martha bustled about, making bread, fixing vegetables, and cooking meat. *Add the figures of Jesus teaching and Mary sitting.*

Martha tried to listen to everything that Jesus said while she worked but it is hard to work and listen at the same time. Finally, she said, "Jesus, I am working hard! Please, tell my sister, Mary, to help me!"

Jesus looked at Martha and said, "Martha, thank you for all the work that you have done. Thank you for taking care of Me and My disciples. You are a good helper. But Mary has chosen to listen to My teaching—and that too is a good choice. You can help Me best by listening now. Please sit down." *Take down the figure of Martha working. Add the figure of Martha sitting.*

Martha sat down and listened to Jesus. She knew that sometimes good helpers have to work and sometimes they have to listen. She wanted to help Jesus so she listened. Later, she knew, everyone would help her make supper. People who follow Jesus are good helpers.

Bible Memory Verse

Help one another in love.

Galatians 5:13 (NIV)

Dear Parent(s),

"Please help!" "Please help pick up the toys, please help set the table, please help your sister." Helpfulness is the service to God, family, and community that makes life both bearable and enjoyable. You ask your child to help you and others every day. This month our class will learn how Martha was helpful in preparing the house and meal for her Lord's visit. Learning to be helpful, like Martha, shouldn't stop at the classroom door. I invite you to share this lesson with your child at home by reading the story of Martha and Mary from a preschool Bible, trying the activities suggested in this letter, and learning this Bible memory verse.

Help one another in love. *Galatians 5:13*

On _____ we will be making a snack to share. This is an opportunity to practice helpfulness and sharing. Please help your child contribute to this activity by bringing:

____ graham crackers   ___ cereal

____ peanut butter   ____ plastic knives

____ nuts   ____ s mall paper plates

____ raisins   ____ small disposable bowls

to our classroom by _____. Thank you for your helpfulness.

Encouragement and appreciation go a long way toward developing helpfulness in your child. It's useful to understand how children are helpful at different ages so you can design successful helping tasks and nurture pride in being helpful.

How Children Learn to Help

Age 3: A 3-year-old loves to imitate. He will stand at the chalkboard and help his teacher erase chalk marks. He will follow mom around the yard with his own plastic rake as mom puts fallen leaves in a pile. And he swishes a sponge in soapy water next to Dad at the sink as they wash dishes together. He will help alongside someone who provides companionship and shows him how a task is done. Instead of expecting him to "Put your toys away," you will get better results with, "Please help put your blocks away. I'll pick up the red blocks, you put the blue blocks in the basket." At 3, your child is learning the "how tos" of helping. 3-year-olds must also begin to hear about the rules of helping; they won't usually follow rules on their own, but will imitate someone who is practicing the rules. "After lunch we put the dishes in the sink. Please come and help me with this task." "While baby naps, we play quietly. Thank you for helping me let baby rest."

Age 4: At 4 it is easier to help, cooperate, and share than it was at 3. 4-year-olds are less possessive, understanding that sharing does not mean losing the object forever. At 4, she has learned many of the steps necessary to complete a task and has the intellectual, emotional, and physical ability to accomplish the task. If you tell her, "Please help, it's your turn to put the dishes in the sink," she's seen you do it, practiced it with your help, and knows the steps required to put dishes in the sink. Now she's ready to do the task herself. At 4, she wants to "do it myself," and her definition of "helpful" may sometimes be exasperating to you. To avoid struggles over who is "helping" whom and what is really "helpful," introduce the process of bargaining/negotiating. If she wants to be helpful and prepare breakfast herself, expect and accept cereal outside of the bowl (she can clean it up with the cordless vacuum later). You can help by pouring milk from the carton into a small pitcher that is easy for her to manage. 4-year-olds are often frustrated when they try to do something "by myself" and can't quite get it right. This is a good time to teach that asking for help is good, just as Martha asked for help from Mary and Jesus.

Age 5: 5-year-olds have a great desire to be helpful, please others, and receive acceptance. A 5-year-old will offer to do something helpful on his own and then report his accomplishment to earn praise and feel proud of himself. This is a great age to introduce Helping Charts with sticker rewards for completing helpful tasks. 5-year-olds follow rules as a way to organize and understand their life and environment. He will be helpful in order to follow an established rule. "At recess, we stand quietly in a straight line, it's the rule." "On Mondays, I empty the wastebaskets, it's the rule." "I make my bed before I eat breakfast, it's the rule." You can praise him for his helpfulness when he follows the rules.

Parent's Prayer

> Heavenly Father, in my efforts to be helpful like Martha, I often get caught up in busy-ness. Martha was very busy preparing for Jesus' visit, trying to do it all, not asking for help until she was overwhelmed, and believing that it was more important to make physical preparations for her Lord than to have her heart prepared by listening to His Word. Father, I often need help as I teach my child. Help me remember to have my heart prepared by Your Word as thoroughly as I prepare my household and business. I ask for Your guidance as I plant the seeds of helpfulness in my child. In Jesus' name I pray. Amen.

Together in Christ,

Family Activities

Martha's Pizza: A Cooking Adventure

Ingredients
1 pizza crust, either homemade or prepared
Pizza sauce
Mozzarella cheese
Favorite toppings: pepperoni, sausage, olives, mushrooms, peppers, onions, etc.
Large wooden spoon
Pizza pan

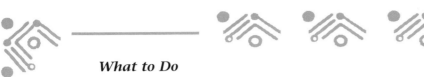

What to Do

1. Assemble all the needed ingredients.
2. Prepare the pizza crust. Prebake if necessary.
3. Chop up the toppings and grate the cheese.
4. Call your child into the kitchen. Help him wash his hands.
5. Using the wooden spoon, help your child spread the pizza sauce over the crust.
6. Let him sprinkle the mozzarella cheese over the crust and put on the toppings.
7. Bake the pizza.
8. Eat and enjoy!

Teaching Helpfulness

- You are modeling helping. Be aware that your child sees your actions and will copy them.
- While eating the pizza, compliment your child for his helpfulness in the kitchen. Remind him that Martha too helped in the kitchen. Preparing this meal for the family is like Martha preparing her meal for the disciples—but they didn't eat pizza!
- There are many ways to be a helper: cleaning up dishes, saying "please" and "thank you," taking turns putting on toppings, following your directions, and so on. Recognize the many ways that your child helped during this meal and praise him for his help.

Sock Swoop: A Move-Around Activity

Materials Needed

- 6 or 10 pairs of socks, rolled into balls
- Laundry basket
- Play area

What to Do

1. Assemble all the needed materials. (Hint: If you wait until laundry day, you will find that these materials will magically assemble themselves!)
2. Toss the balled-up socks around the play area.
3. Have the child run to pick up the sock balls and to put them in the laundry basket.
4. Demonstrate how to swoop instead of stopping.
5. Call out directions ("Pick up the green socks!") to encourage listening skills.

Teaching Helpfulness

- This activity combines what Martha did (bustle about the house) with what Mary did (listen to instructions). Either of them could have chosen to do what the other did or they could have each done both. Both are ways of helping Jesus.

- Paul tells us that faith, which comes from hearing (Romans 10:17), is dead without works (James 2:17). Here you have a chance to help your child understand what it means to put instruction into action.

- Praise your child for helping you clean up the play area and finish your laundry task. Explain how much easier life is when the home is full of good helpers.

Help Getting Dressed: A Getting-Organized Activity

Materials Needed
- Large piece of cardboard
- Pencil
- Crayons
- Scissors or box cutter
- Tomorrow's clothes

What to Do
1. Have your child lie down on the cardboard. Trace her outline. Cut it out with the scissors or the box cutter.
2. Help your child color the self-portrait.
3. Select tomorrow's clothes. Dress the doll—or just lay the clothes on top of it. Be sure to place each piece of clothing in the right place.
4. The next morning, encourage your child to dress herself, using the doll as a guide.

Teaching Helpfulness
- Your child can use this doll as a guide to get herself dressed, thus making the day easier for you. Thank your child for being such a good helper!
- As you and your child color the doll, help her tell the story of Martha and Jesus. What did Martha do? What did Jesus do? How did Martha help Jesus? Can your child help you—or Jesus—in the same ways?

Easy Stuff
1. Include your child in daily household tasks, unloading groceries, folding laundry, feeding pets. Praise him for his help.
2. Point out examples of helpful behaviors on your child's favorite TV programs. Can't find any? Maybe another program would be a better choice.
3. Remind your child that manners are essential to making your home and the community a pleasant place to live. Make sure he hears you say "please" and "thank you" to grocery store clerks, restaurant servers, and bank tellers.

Let's Listen!

Mary Listens to Jesus

Bible Memory Verse

Be quick to listen, slow to speak.
James 1:19

Teacher's Prayer

Heavenly Father, how can I teach the children in my care to listen when I so often get caught up in giving instructions, talking, and reprimanding that I forget to listen to them? You gave me two ears and one mouth, that I should listen twice as much as I speak. Help me remember to be more like Mary, listening to the children in my care and to Your Word. Thank You for the gift of hearing. Let me use it to listen to the children in my care the way You listen to me—patiently, attentively, and constantly. In Jesus' name I pray. Amen.

Teaching Objective: Listening

To help children improve their listening skills, just as Mary listened at the feet of Jesus.

Through God's Word and the power of the Holy Spirit, by the end of this unit, the children should be able to:

1. Tell the basic story of Mary and Martha.
2. Repeat the Bible memory verse.
3. Comprehend the teaching objective *listening*.
4. Show an increased ability to listen.
5. Listen quietly to a story.

Learning to listen takes practice. In addition to hearing the words, we have to understand them, remember them, and do what is communicated. You can help the children learn to listen, remember, and act by first understanding and remembering how children listen at different ages.

How Preschoolers Learn to Listen

Age 3: Listening leads to language development. 3-year-olds learn to listen by having lots of language to listen to. The best way to teach listening is to talk, read, and sing to the children. 3-year-olds ask "why" questions as a way to start conversation and gather information. You can start to teach the children the art of conversation but you'll be the one responsible for keeping the ideas flowing back and forth. Read a book together and talk about what the characters did. A 3-year-old may insist on hearing a story read over and over again because she learns when she listens to things repeatedly. You can teach instructions, rules, and facts through repetition too. Devise simple phrases to describe rules and repeat them often: "We'll line up straight and tall before we walk down the hall." 3-year-olds are practicing listening and working hard to understand what the words mean but are not always ready or able to act on what they hear and understand. They need lots of patience and prompting from you.

Age 4: 4-year-olds want to be praised and complimented for their accomplishments. A 4-year-old will gladly listen to any positive words you offer, so even when you must reprimand or enforce a rule, try to word it in a positive way: "It was hard for you to share the toys today, you'll do better tomorrow." 4-year-olds have great fun with language, especially rhymes and silly words. Use rhymes and silly words to get his attention, but don't expect immediate action—at 4 he's still practicing the follow-through.

Teach listening by being a good listener. Practice patience by giving a child your full attention when he talks to you. At 4 he'll ask "why" questions constantly—a sure sign that he wants to listen and attempt a two-way conversation. But beware the "whys" that are stall tactics: "Why do I have to put on my shoes? Why are the stones on the ground? Why will stones hurt my feet?"

Age 5: Listening can be quite tiring. The 5-year-old listens to parents, siblings, teachers, friends, and TV all day long. She can now carry on a conversation and often lengthy monologs about the activities of her day or an elaborate fantasy tale. It's important to balance talking and listening with quiet time, for both child and adult. Remember that when your eyes glaze over there's been too much talk and too little quiet. At 5, a child's "why" questions are a true search for information and understanding. Keep answers short—a lengthy, detailed explanation is "white noise" to her.

Teaching Activities

Decorate the Bible Memory Verse: Musical Interlude

Materials Needed

- Copies of the Bible memory verse (page 85), one per child
- Any type of art materials: paints, crayons, chalk, markers, etc.
- Emotional music, your choice

What to Do

1. To decorate this unit's Bible memory verse, the children will color in response to music. Care should be taken in selecting the music—it should evoke feelings and inspire creativity. Choose instrumentals. This will enable the children to respond to what they hear in the music rather than what they hear in lyrics.

2. Before school starts, set up for this project as you would any group art project. Make sure that each child will have ample work space and access to the materials. Put one copy of the Bible memory verse at each child's place. This activity will require a great deal of adult supervision.

3. Settle the children into their work areas. Remind them how to properly use the art materials. Explain that they will listen to the music, just as Mary listened to Jesus, and create a response to it on their papers. Turn the music on and let them work away.

Teaching Listening

- While the children are working, approach them individually to discuss what they hear in the music and how they are conveying that on their page. Be careful, however, not to disturb any child deeply engaged in his work. Let them listen to the music and respond to it now; they can listen to you later.

- Read the Bible memory verse to each child. Ask them for ways that they can be quick to listen and slow to speak. Model appropriate listening skills by facing each child, looking into her eyes, and using nonverbal encouragement.

- Remind children to share, just like Noah. Encourage them to follow directions, just like Jonah. Let them help you, just like Martha. All require that they use their listening skills.

- Encourage the children to work quietly, saving their words for an appropriate time. Even Moses knew when to stop talking and listen to God.

Keeping the Teaching Objective Alive in the Classroom: Mary's Listening Spot

Materials Needed

- A child-friendly tape recorder with head-phones
- Several books on tape and the corre-sponding books
- A cozy spot for listening

What to Do

1. Arrange this area of your classroom so it is conducive to quiet listening. As each child shows interest, teach her how to use the tape recorder and head phones.

2. Vary the recorded books in the listening center. You might want to make some of your own tapes while reading to the class during Circle Time. If parents send in books, be sure to include those too.

Teaching Listening

- When the children use Mary's Listening Spot, praise them. Encourage them to use the materials correctly and thought-fully.

- After each book, ask the children what the book was about. Encourage them to tell you what they heard. Ask them to identify the "turn the page" signal. Did they listen for it?

- If conflicts arise in the listening center, remind the children to share, as Noah did, and to use their words, as Moses did. Remind them also that they must listen to one another so everyone will get a chance to use the books.

Listen! Listen!: A Circle-Time Game to Teach Listening

Materials Needed

- Your voice

What to Do

1. During Circle Time, in a whisper, tell the children to raise their arms when they hear their name.

2. One at a time, whisper each child's name. Silently applaud each person who lifts his or her arms.

3. Expand this game to simply listen to the environmental sounds. Help the children name what they hear.

Teaching Listening

- This game helps the children become more aware of the different sounds in their environment. As they wait for their names to be called, they will hear differ-ent noises. They must learn to pick out your voice from the background noise.

- This game also fosters self-control, as each child must keep very still and quiet in order to hear the names. An extra benefit is that this game has a calming effect on the children.

- Jesus called Martha and Mary by name. God called Moses, Jonah, and Noah by their names too. Remind the children that they must listen for their names, spoken by you or by God. As they sit quietly, pause to let them listen to God; perhaps He is calling their names too.

Hear My Heart?: A Craft Project to Teach Listening

Materials Needed

- Cardboard tubes
- Scissors
- Yarn
- Hole punch
- Construction paper
- Glue or glue sticks

What to Do

1. Cut the cardboard tubes into 2″ sections. You will need one section per child. Cut one 18″ piece of yarn per child.

2. Before school starts, set up as you would for any other art project. This project will require adult assistance. Set out the tubes, yarn, hole punch, construction paper, and glue.

3. Help the children punch holes on opposite sides of their tubes. Help them thread the yarn through the holes. Tie it together.

4. Show the children how to tear the construction paper into small pieces. Have them glue the small pieces onto the tube.

5. When the tubes are dry, show the children how to listen to a friend's heartbeat by placing one end of the tube on the friend's chest and the other end up to their own ear.

Teaching Listening

• As the children tear the paper, help them listen to the noise. Is there a special noise from the hole punch? What about the sound of putting the glue on the tube? Talk about the various noises that you hear as you make the craft.

• Do they hear the heartbeats? Hearts help us to feel love for our friends. Tell the children that Jesus loved Mary and Martha; He loves each child in the class as well. Remind them of this fact. Tell them also that Jesus listens carefully to each child's prayers.

• Are the children sharing the materials? If not, urge them to remember Noah. Are they using their words? If not, remember Moses. Did they follow directions? Remember Jonah! Are they helping each other? Remember Martha!

Listening Pairs: An Activity to Teach Listening

Materials Needed

• 8–12 clean, empty yogurt cups and covers

• Assorted noise-making items: sugar, cotton balls, beans, water, coins

• 4–6 pairs of matching stickers

• Glue

What to Do

1. Divide the yogurt cups into pairs. Into each pair, put the same noisemakers. On the bottom of each pair, put matching stickers. Glue the lids shut.

2. Introduce this activity as you would any new learning center. Teach the children to match the pairs by shaking and listening. Show them how to use the stickers to self-check their work.

Teaching Listening

• This activity is based on listening. When the children select it, praise them for choosing to listen, just like Mary did.

• Focus on the number of sounds they were able to match. Praise them for listening carefully and distinguishing the sounds.

• Ask them to guess what they think is making each noise. If they guess correctly, congratulate them for listening so carefully.

Loud or Quiet: A Manipulative to Teach Listening

Materials Needed

• Copies of the Loud or Quiet Matching Squares (pages 86–89)

• Scissors

• Four sheets of heavy white paper

- Glue
- Red and blue markers
- Three small baskets (berry baskets work well)
- Red ribbon
- Blue ribbon

What to Do

1. Make copies of the Loud or Quiet Matching Squares.

2. Glue all the Matching Squares to heavy white paper. When the squares are dry, cut along the dotted lines. On the backs of the Loud Sound Squares (pages 88–89), draw a simple shape with the red marker. On the backs of the Quiet Sound Squares (pages 86–87), draw a simple shape with the blue marker. At this point, you may choose to laminate them.

3. Tie the red and blue ribbons on two separate baskets. Put the finished squares into the third small basket.

4. Introduce this activity as you would any new learning center. Show the children how to sort the squares into the Loud Basket (red ribbon) or the Quiet Basket (blue ribbon).

5. When they have finished sorting, show them how to self-check their work by using the colored shape on the back of the Sound Square.

Teaching Listening

- This activity requires that the children sit still and learn. Praise them for choosing to do what Mary did.

- As they work, talk to the children about loud and quiet noises. Ask them which they prefer. Ask them what they like to listen to. Have them make some of the noises. Which ones do they think Mary would have heard?

- Remember, preschoolers love repetition. If appropriate, repeat any of the praises or suggestions for Teaching Listening described elsewhere in this unit.

Mary's Song: A Circle-Time Game to Teach the Bible Memory Verse

Materials Needed

- A copy of the Bible memory verse (page 85)

What to Do

1. Lead the children in singing Mary's Song to the tune of "Frère Jacques":

   Be quick to listen; Quick to listen.
   Slow to speak; Slow to speak.
   James 1:19; James 1:19.
   Touch your head; Touch your head.

2. Change the last line, giving a variety of simple directions: hug a friend, clap your hands, jump up high, and so on.

Teaching Listening

- This song combines repetition of the Bible memory verse with listening for directions. Active listening produces strong memories.

- Praise the children for hearing and following the directions in the last two lines of the song. Encourage those who ignore your directions to pay better attention.

Music Makers: An Activity to Teach the Bible Memory Verse

Materials Needed

- Stiff paper plates, two per child
- Beans or other noisemakers
- Staples and stapler
- Copies of the Bible Memory Verse Tambourine (page 90), one per child

- Markers or crayons
- Child-sized scissors
- Glue

What to Do

1. Set up for this activity as you would any art project.

2. Have the children put a small handful of beans in the center of one of the stiff plates. Put the second plate on top. Staple the two plates together.

3. Have children draw a circle or other shape around the Bible memory verse on the Bible Memory Verse Tambourine page. The shape should fit on the tambourine plates.

4. Using crayons or markers, have the children decorate the Bible memory verse shape. Help them cut out the shape and glue it onto their tambourines.

5. Let the tambourines dry.

6. Use them to make a joyful noise unto the Lord while singing Mary's Song or any other appropriate Circle-Time music.

Teaching Listening

- Allow the children to do as much of this process as they can: stapling, cutting, gluing. All provide opportunities for them to listen to your guidance and learn.

- Read the Bible memory verse to the children. Help them repeat it back to you. Ask them to think about what it means. Ask them about Mary—was she quick to listen?

- Listen carefully to the chatter going on as the children work on this project. Encourage them to listen to each other. Praise them for having conversations rather than monologs.

- Vary the items in the tambourines. Encourage the children to listen and to hear the different sounds.

Telling the Story

Before you begin

To tell the story for this unit, have the children stand in a circle around you. Whenever they hear the word *listen* (or *listening* or *listened* or any form of the word), they are to take one step toward you. Soon they will be sitting at your feet, just as Mary sat at the feet of Jesus. Read the story in bold print; the instructions are italicized.

Before I tell today's Bible story, everyone please form a large circle around me. *Pause until the children are ready.* **Please stand up.** *Pause.* **Now, you must listen very carefully to this story. When you hear me say the word *listen*, take a step toward me. When you get close to me, you may sit down near my feet. Ready to practice? On what word do you take a step forward?** *Wait for the children to respond correctly. Supply the answer if needed.* **I hear the bell.** *Check to be sure that no one moves.* **Look! There is a book.** *No one should move.* **Let's *listen* to the story.** *Make sure everyone takes one step into the circle.*

God made people to live in families. Even Jesus lived in a family; some people believe that he had brothers and sisters. Today, some of us have brothers and some of us have sisters. Let's *listen* to a story about two sisters, both were friends of Jesus. *Make sure everyone takes one step into the circle.* **Their names were Martha and Mary.**

One morning, Martha looked out her front door and saw Jesus and His disciples coming toward her house. Martha began to get the house ready for the visit. She called

to her sister, "Mary! I need your help. We must get ready for Jesus!" Mary came to Martha right away because she could *listen* very well. *Make sure everyone takes one step into the circle.* Quickly, Martha told Mary what needed to be done. Mary *listened*, nodded her head, and the two of them scurried about, getting ready for Jesus and His disciples.

When Jesus arrived, He greeted both sisters with a kiss. Martha went back to work, but Mary sat down with Jesus. She wanted to *listen* to all that He had to teach. *Make sure everyone takes one step into the circle.* Jesus taught and taught while Mary sat and heard His words. He was a good teacher. She was a good student.

After a while, Martha came into the room. She said, "Jesus, I am working hard! Please, tell my sister, Mary, to help me!"

Mary was surprised—she knew how important it was to *listen* to Jesus when He talked. *Make sure everyone takes one step into the circle.* What could Martha be complaining about?

Jesus looked at Martha and said, "Martha, thank you for all the work that you have done. You are a good helper. But Mary has chosen to *listen* to My teaching—and that was the best choice. *Make sure everyone takes one step into the circle.* You can help Me best by *listening* now. *Make sure everyone takes one step into the circle.* "Please sit down." *Encourage the children to sit down. By now, they should have reached your feet.*

So Martha sat down with Mary, and together they listened to all that Jesus had to say. Mary smiled because she knew that all of Jesus' friends were good listeners.

Bible Memory Verse

Be quick to listen, slow to speak.

James 1:19 (NIV)

Loud or Quiet Matching Squares

Rabbit

Wind

Bird

Clock

Bell

Mouse

Loud or Quiet Matching Squares

Children whispering

Kitten

Book (library voices)

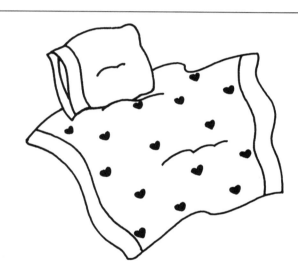

Pillow and blanket

Children drawing pictures

Flower

Loud or Quiet Matching Squares

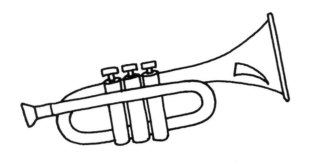

Trumpet

Drum

Large bell

Alarm clock

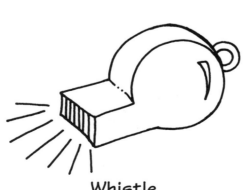

Whistle

Roaring lion

Loud or Quiet Matching Squares

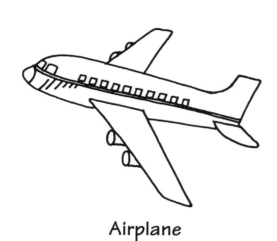

Airplane

train

Children playing kick ball

Hammer hitting nail

Lawn mower

Children yelling

Bible Memory Verse Tambourine

Be quick to listen, slow to speak.

James 1:19 (NIV)

Dear Parent(s),

"Please listen!" It's exasperating to repeat yourself over and over when your child doesn't listen. Learning to listen is an important part of gaining knowledge and following directions. Mary sat quietly and patiently at Jesus' feet, listening to Him teach. This month, our class will learn about Mary and how she listened. You can help our class practice listening by recording yourself reading a favorite children's book on a cassette tape and sending it to school with your child. You may send as many stories as you'd like—15-minute tapes, one story per side, work best.

The lessons of Mary shouldn't stop at the classroom door. I invite you to share these listening lessons with your child at home by reading the story of Mary from a preschool Bible, trying the activities suggested in this letter, and teaching this Bible memory verse.

Be quick to listen, slow to speak. *James 1:19*

Learning to listen takes patience and practice. You can help your child learn to listen by first understanding how children listen at different ages.

How Preschoolers Learn to Listen

Age 3: Listening leads to language development. 3-year-olds learn to listen by having lots of language to listen to. The best way to teach listening is to talk, read, and sing to your child. 3-year-olds ask "why" questions as a way to start conversation and gather information. You can start to teach your child the art of conversation but you'll be the one responsible for keeping the ideas flowing back and forth. Read a book together and talk about what the characters did. She may insist on hearing a story read over and over again because she learns when she listens to things repeatedly. You can teach instructions, rules, and facts through repetition too. Make up simple phrases to describe rules and repeat them often: "Clothes on my body there must be before I can watch morning TV." "I brush my teeth every day to chase away tooth decay." "Make my bed in the morning, and tonight I will be snoring." 3-year-olds are practicing listening and working hard to understand what the words mean but are not always ready or able to act on what they hear and understand. They need lots of patience and prompting from you.

Age 4: 4-year-olds want to be praised and complimented for their accomplishments. Your 4-year-old will gladly listen to any positive words you offer, so even when you must reprimand or enforce a rule, try to word it in a positive way. "It was hard for you to share the toys today, you'll do better tomorrow." 4-year-olds have great fun with language, especially rhymes and silly words. Use rhymes and silly words to get his attention, but don't expect immediate action—at 4 he's still practicing the follow-through. Teach listening by being a good listener. Practice patience and give your child your full attention when he talks to you. At 4 he'll ask "why" questions constantly—a sure sign that he wants to listen and attempt a two-way conversation. But beware the "whys" that are stall tactics: "Why do I have to put on my shoes? Why are the stones on the ground? Why will stones hurt my feet?"

Age 5: Listening can be quite tiring. 5-year-olds listen to parents, siblings, teachers, friends, and TV all day long. Your 5-year-old can now carry on a conversation and often lengthy monologs about the activities of her day or an elaborate fantasy tale. It's important to balance talking and listening with quiet time, for both child and adult. Remember that when your eyes glaze over there's been too much talk and too little quiet. At 5, a child's "why" questions are a true search for information and understanding. Keep answers short—a lengthy, detailed explanation is "white noise" to your child.

As you try so hard to teach your child to listen to you and to others, you may forget to take the time to listen to your child. As you struggle to open your ears and listen to your child, turn to your heavenly Father in prayer and listen to your child as He listens to you—patiently, without argument, and always in love.

Parent's Prayer

Heavenly Father, how can I teach my child to listen when I so often get caught up in giving instructions, talking, and reprimanding that I forget to listen to her? You gave me two ears and one mouth that I should listen twice as much as I speak. Help me remember to be more like Mary, stopping to listen to my child and Your Word. Thank You for the gift of hearing. Let me use it to listen to my child the way that You listen to me—patiently, attentively, and constantly.

Together in Christ,

Family Activities

Ssssh and Pop: A Quiet and Noisy Cooking Adventure

Ingredients
- Popcorn
- Popcorn popper, microwave oven, hot oil popper, or air popper

What to Do
1. Look at the unpopped popcorn. Listen.
2. Pop the popcorn. Listen.
3. Eat the popcorn. Listen.

Teaching Listening

- This snack has a quiet sound (before popping) and a loud sound (during popping). As you make this treat, listen to the sounds. Talk about what you hear.

- As you prepare this snack with your child, make an effort to read the instructions aloud. Help your child listen to what you read and follow your directions. Remind her to "Listen! Listen!" as you read aloud—just as Mary listened and learned from Jesus.

- At each point in the preparation of this snack, talk about the different noises that the ingredients and tools make. Try pouring the popcorn into bowls made of different materials (plastic, metal, glass). How does the sound change in each bowl?

Listen! Listen!: A Move-Around Activity

Materials Needed

- A loud clock, kitchen timer, music box, or tape recorder

What to Do

1. Set aside a time to play this game that will be relatively quite. Turn off the TV and stereo, close the windows. Explain to your child how to play the game.

2. Tell your child to cover his eyes. Hide the noisy toy someplace in the playing area. Make sure that it is making its noise.

3. Once the toy is hidden, ask your child to open his eyes. Encourage him to listen for the toy's sound and then find the toy by following its sounds.

4. Reverse roles: he hides, you find.

Teaching Listening

- To successfully play this game, your child must master his excitement long enough to listen carefully. Then, he must identify where the noisy toy is hidden. In addition to improving listening skills, this game also teaches your child self-control. Be sure to comment on his attempts at self-discipline.

- Put the emphasis of this game on the listening rather than on the finding. Focus on improving ability to hear the sound; praise him for choosing to listen just as Mary did.

- Try hiding toys with different sound volumes—some louder, some quieter.

- Ask your child about the story of Mary. Who talked? Who listened? How did Mary listen? What did she do while she was listening? How can we be like Mary?

Same or Different: Fun with Rhythms

Materials Needed

- Pairs of noise-making instruments: tin cans, oatmeal boxes, glasses of water, or a purchased musical toy
- Pairs of sticks, wooden spoons, or pencils for banging

What to Do

1. Give your child a noise-making instrument and a banging stick. Keep the other instrument and banging stick for yourself.
2. Play a distinct rhythm on the instrument. Encourage your child to try to copy your rhythm. Reverse the roles. Increase or decrease the complexity of the rhythm, depending on your child's ability.
3. Play two rhythms. Ask your child to tell you if they are the same or different. Reverse roles.

Teaching Listening

- Mary had to listen carefully to Jesus' teaching. In the same way, you and your child must listen carefully to the rhythms to be able to copy them.
- Delight in your child's successes. Praise her for listening so carefully to your rhythms. Thrill to her creative rhythms. Jesus was delighted with Mary too because she had chosen to listen.

Easy Stuff

1. Increase listening skills by asking your child questions about bedtime stories as you read them.
2. Listen to music and repeat the lyrics. Can you remember what you just heard? Can you sing the song?
3. While waiting in line at the post office, at the grocery store, or in the clinic waiting room, encourage your child to listen to the sounds around her. Help her label them. Point out faint sounds and encourage her to listen carefully to hear them.

Tell the Truth!

John the Baptist Speaks God's Word

Bible Memory Verse

The Lord hates … a lying tongue.
Proverbs 6:16–17

Teacher's Prayer

Heavenly Father, John spoke the truth—the truth about Christ our Savior. Each day I have the opportunity to teach Your truth to the children in my care just as John taught Your truths to the crowds at the river. Please guide me as I teach Your Word and teach about truth by my example. Keep my tongue from telling little lies of convenience, answering questions less than truthfully, and asking others to lie on my behalf. I need Your help to walk a straight path and guide the children in my care away from crooked roads. In Jesus' name I pray. Amen.

Teaching Objective: Truthfulness

To help the children understand what "the truth" is and help them learn to tell the truth faithfully, just as John the Baptist faithfully and truthfully spoke the Word of God.

Through God's Word and the power of the Holy Spirit, by the end of this unit, the children should be able to:

1. Tell the basic story of John the Baptist.

2. Repeat the Bible memory verse.

3. Comprehend the teaching objective *truthfulness*.

4. Show an increased ability to tell the truth.

5. Identify the difference between true and false statements, and real and pretend situations.

The way children lie, and the reasons they do so, change as they grow. As preschoolers, their thoughts and words are a mixture of fantasy, desire, misunderstanding, and a desire to please others while not getting into trouble themselves. You can help the children "speak the truth" and establish early patterns that discourage lying by understanding and remembering how children learn to tell the truth at different ages and stages of development.

How Children Learn to Tell the Truth

Age 3: 3-year-olds rarely lie to deceive, but they may tell quite a few untruths. Your 3-year-old has a vivid imagination and may tell fantastic stories that certainly are not true but neither are they lies. When a child tells you that the pet rabbit in your classroom can talk, you might say, "We know rabbits can't really talk, but wouldn't it be fun if they could?" You can help him separate fantasy from reality while still encouraging his creative imagination. Sometimes 3-year-olds lie to test rules. A child says he didn't ride his trike into the street to see if you will enforce the "stay on the sidewalk" rule. You can firmly state that you know he broke the rule and now must lose his trike-riding privilege for the rest of the morning. This teaches him that you know he broke a rule, that you consistently enforce rules, and that what he did was wrong, without confusing him with the concept of lying. This is a good age to give praise for telling the truth rather than focusing on lies. 3-year-olds will often come and tell you that they have broken a rule or caused an accident. When he tells you that he has spilled the milk, react calmly, help him clean it up, and tell him that you appreciate his truthfulness. He will learn to trust you and be more likely to tell you the truth as he grows up.

Age 4: 4-year-olds still have trouble telling fact from fiction and may tell a lie because they wish something were true. "I didn't break the vase" means "I didn't mean for it to get broken and I wish it hadn't happened." You can help 4-year-old children learn to tell the truth by asking questions that encourage truthfulness. When you know she broke the vase, you can say, "You were bouncing your ball in the classroom and the ball hit the vase. Now it's broken." Teach her about honesty by being honest yourself. Tell her the truth, "It will seem like a long morning on your first day at preschool, and you might feel sad, but your mom will come back to pick you up right after snack time."

Age 5: 5-year-olds try to tell the truth but aren't always successful. A 5-year-old child will lie to protect himself from punishment. You can help 5-year-olds tell the truth by making it easy to admit wrongdoing. Avoid setting him up to lie by asking, "Did you take the truck?" Tell him, "I saw you take the truck; it makes me sad when you disobey, now the truck will be in time-out for the rest of the morning." Listen to the child, let him explain the reasons behind his actions. If you understand why he did something wrong, you can help him solve problems in better ways. If he knows that you take the time to listen and care, he is less likely to lie and hide what he did wrong.

Teaching Activities

Decorate the Bible Memory Verse: Wet Work

Materials Needed

- Copies of the Bible memory verse (page 102), one per child
- Powdered tempera paint, 2 or 3 colors
- 2 or 3 shakers, one for each color of paint
- Rain or plant mister filled with water

What to Do

1. Set up for this art project as you normally would. Put the powdered tempera paint in the shakers. Put the shakers, Bible memory verses, and plant mister with water on the work table.

2. Have the children shake a few sprinkles of tempera paint on the Bible memory verse.

3. If it is raining, have the children walk outside with the Bible memory verse for about a minute and let the rain splash the paper and paint. If it is not raining, help each child lightly mist the Bible memory verse and paint with the plant mister.

Teaching Honesty

- Read the Bible memory verse to each child. Help him list examples of lies and truths. Ask what God thought about the lies and the truths.

- After sprinkling the dry paint on the paper, say, "I tell you the truth, the water will change this picture in an amazing way." When it does so, point out your truth. Link this to John's story by reminding the children of the amazing appearance of God's Spirit in the form of the dove.

- Remind the children to share the materials, just as Noah did. Encourage them to use their words to settle disputes, just as Moses did. Help them follow directions, just as Jonah did. Praise them for helping each other, as Martha did. Prompt them to listen to each other, like Mary did. Then tell them that doing all these things will create a more peaceful classroom. I tell you the truth, this will make everyone happier!

Keeping the Teaching Objective Alive in the Classroom: John's Garments

Materials Needed

- Dress-up clothes
- 54" × 12" piece of brown fake fur
- Scissors
- Rope
- Solid color adult-sized T-shirts
- Children's bathrobes

What to Do

1. Make John's camel-hair garment by folding the piece of fur in half lengthwise. Then fold it in half width-wise. Cut a small semicircle from the folded corner. Unfold the garment. This should be a simple tunic with a head hole in the middle. (See diagram.)

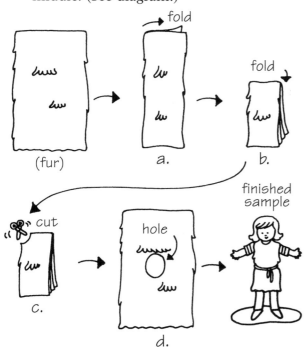

2. Fashion a belt from the rope for the children to pull on over the tunic.

3. Cut the neckline ribbing and the sleeves off the T-shirts. These, combined with the bathrobes, can function as biblical garments.

4. Put the new clothes in your dress-up area.

Teaching Honesty

- Dress-up is a perfect opportunity to talk about real versus pretend, true versus false. As the children pretend to be mothers, fathers, firefighters, nurses, doctors, teachers, pastors, and others, point out that they are still children, just as God really made them to be but they pretend to be grown-ups. Real and pretend, true and false, are difficult concepts for children to grasp. Use every opportunity to explain these differences.

- When a child has chosen the John garment, help him to tell the story of John. What did John do? What did the people ask? What did Jesus say? What was the most important thing that John did?

- Encourage the children to act out the story of John, or any other Bible stories that they have learned. Listen carefully to the dialog. Are they relating the spirit of the story? Do you hear the key phrases: please share, use your words, follow directions, please help, listen, and tell the truth? If so, congratulate yourself because the children have learned to live the Bible's truths. I tell you the truth, some adults have not yet mastered this!

True or False: A Circle-Time Game to Teach Honesty

Materials Needed

- Red and green construction paper
- Black marker
- Scissors

What to Do

1. On the red construction paper, draw a simple, frowning face. Cut it out.

2. On the green construction paper, draw a simple, smiling face. Cut it out.

3. Before Circle Time, put the faces on opposite sides of the circle area.

4. During Circle Time, explain the rules to the children. "I am going to say something. If you think that I am telling the truth, go stand next to the green happy face. If you think that I am not telling the truth, go stand next to the red sad face." Make an obviously true or false statement, then wait for the children to move to their chosen face. Repeat the statement and discuss its trueness. Have the children come back to their places.

5. Repeat the process. Allow each child to have the opportunity to make the true or false statements.

Teaching Honesty

- Be sure to repeat whether the statement is true or false several times. Discuss what makes it the truth or a lie. Help the children give their ideas. Guide them as they develop their understanding of truth.

- Remind the children that God is happy when they tell the truth but He is sad when they lie.

- Jesus said, "I am the truth." If we want to be like Jesus, then we must strive to always speak the truth.

Tell the Truth Rubs: A Craft Project to Teach Honesty

Materials Needed

- Copies of the Tell the Truth Rubs (pages 103–104)

- Card stock, poster board, or other heavy-weight paper
- Pencil
- Scissors
- Envelopes, one for each shape
- Crayons

What to Do

1. Cut out the Tell the Truth Rubs shapes. Use them as patterns to trace the shapes onto the heavy paper. You will need at least one shape per child.

2. Put each shape in a separate envelope. Seal the envelope.

3. Before school starts, set up for this activity as you would any art project; put the crayons and sealed envelopes on the work surface.

4. Using the crayons, show the children how to rub across the envelope, pressing to make the shape that is sealed inside appear.

Teaching Honesty

- Before they start to rub, tell the children, "I tell you the truth, there is something exciting from our story in these envelopes." When the shape appears, remind them that you did indeed tell the truth.

- Help them name the shape in the envelope. Guide them in telling how the shape fits into the story.

- Although the envelope may appear empty, the shape eventually shows up under the rubbing. Lies are like that too—you might not be able to see them at first, but eventually the truth will appear. Plant this idea with the children; in the future, they will reap full understanding of truthfulness.

Truthful Pictures: A Center Activity to Teach the Story

Materials Needed

- Copies of the Truthful Pictures (pages 105–107)
- Contact paper or laminating material
- Dry erase marker
- Dry erase eraser

What to Do

1. Make copies of the Truthful Pictures. Cover them with contact paper or laminate them.
2. For this activity, show the children the papers. Help them cross out the false picture in each pair.
3. Help them check their work.
4. Have them erase their work for the next person.

Teaching Honesty

- In each pair, talk about which picture is true and which is false. Help the children understand and verbalize the difference.
- If you notice that they have changed an answer, ask why. Praise them for being honest with you about any changes they made.
- Notice the children's behavior in this center. Are they sharing? Using their words? Following directions? Helping each other? Praise them for their efforts to live like the Bible characters: "Justin, I tell you the truth, you are acting just like Noah when you share the pencils."

Baptizing Like John: A Center Activity to Teach the Story

Materials Needed

- Water play table
- Washable dolls
- Towels

What to Do

1. Set up the water play table and dolls as you normally would.
2. As the children wash the dolls, talk to them about Baptism. Say, "I see you are washing your dolls and getting all the dirt off them. When a person is baptized, God washes them clean from their sins."
3. Help the children dry off the dolls.

Teaching Honesty

- If full submersion is different from your church's tradition of Baptism, talk to the children about this difference.
- Explain the significance of Baptism in your church, no matter what method is used. Explain why it is important for all believers to be baptized.
- Link this activity to the story. Be sure to explain that John baptized real people while the child is only washing pretend babies. Real and pretend, true and false, repetition helps drive these concepts home.

Lying Tongue Trap: A Circle-Time Game to Teach the Bible Memory Verse

Materials Needed

- A copy of the Bible memory verse (page 102)

What to Do

1. Lead the children in singing "John's Song" to the tune of "London Bridge."

   The Lord hates a lying tongue,
   Lying tongue, lying tongue.
   The Lord hates a lying tongue.
   Proverbs 6:26.

2. This game is played like "London Bridge." Two children join hands to form the bridge and other children walk under the bridge while singing "John's Song."

3. After the last line, the bridge drops and traps one child.

4. Make a clearly true statement ("I am a person.") or a clearly false one ("I am a cow."). The trapped child has to tell whether the statement is true or false. Let the children forming the bridge try making statements too. Switch positions.

5. Continue until all the children have had a chance to judge true from false.

Teaching Honesty

• Praise the children when they distinguish true from false statements.

• Use obviously false or true statements until the children begin to understand the difference. Then begin to make the statements more difficult to judge. For example, the statement "I am a cow" is obviously false but "I am wearing a blue skirt" when you have on blue pants requires more sophisticated judgment.

• Be sure to include true and false statements from the Bible story: "John baptized Jesus." "Jesus baptized John." "John baptized people with sand." "John wore a garment made from camel's hair."

• When most of the children have been captured, ask for a show of hands of who has not been captured. Encourage the children to answer honestly!

Lying Tongue Masks: A Craft Project to Teach the Bible Memory Verse

Materials Needed

• Copies of the Lying Tongues (page 108), one per child

• Paper plates, one per child

• Scissors

• Pencil

• Yarn

• Crayons, markers, glitter, paper, paints, etc.

• Glue

What to Do

1. Make copies of the Lying Tongues. You might want to copy them onto various colors of paper. Cut them out.

2. Draw eyeholes in the paper plates. Cut them out.

3. Cut yarn into 12″ lengths, two per mask. Poke holes in the paper plates next to the eyeholes. Tie one piece of yarn in each hole.

4. Before school starts, set this project up as you normally would.

5. Instruct the children to decorate the masks with the art supplies.

6. For the last step, have them glue the Lying Tongue to the mask. Let them glue it anywhere that they want.

7. Use yarn to tie the mask on the children.

Teaching Honesty

• Read the Bible memory verse written on the tongues to the children. Help them repeat the verse, including its reference.

• Ask them to explain what a lie is. Ask for examples. Ask the children to explain the truth to you. Ask for an example. Correct their explanations and examples when necessary.

• Comment on where they have placed the tongue.

• Are the children sharing? Using their words? Following directions? Helping one another? Listening? If so, praise them. If not, make positive comments to get them back on track: "Abbey, I tell you the truth, it is better to share the glue."

Telling the Story

Before you begin

To tell the story this unit, you will use the shapes from Tell the Truth Rubs (pages 103–104) and a flannel board. Use the rub shapes as patterns; cut the shapes from a heavy-weight paper such as card stock or poster board. Color the shapes as desired. Place small pieces of Velcro brand adhesive or rolls of tape on the back of each shape. Read the story written in bold; the instructions are italicized.

God's Word is called the Bible. *Put the book shape on the flannel board.* **People wrote the Bible, but God made sure that everything in it is the truth. Prophets, who are a little bit like preachers, used to walk around cities and countries, proclaiming God's Word and its truth. Once, there was such a prophet named John—he was Jesus' cousin.** *Take down the book shape and put up the John figure.* **John lived in the desert. He wore a tunic made from camel hair, tied with a rope. He ate honey and locust. This is the truth that he told to people:**

"Prepare the way for the Lord, make straight paths for Him. The crooked roads will become straight." *Place the crooked shape on the board. Cover it with the straight shape.* **"All of the people will see God's salvation."**

When the crowds heard this, they were frightened. *Add the crowd shape.* **They wanted the Lord to know that they loved Him so they asked John, "What should we do?"**

John said, "You should share. The one who has two tunics should share with his friend." Do you remember this Bible memory verse? We learned it when we talked about Noah. **"And you must be honest with taxes and money. Don't collect more than your share. Don't steal from people. And when someone asks you what happened, tell the truth. The Lord hates it when you lie. If you are willing to do all these hard things, if you want to repent from your old, bad ways, then come and be baptized in the Jordan river."** *Remove the crooked and straight shapes, and add the water shape.*

The people eagerly came into the river, and John baptized them. *Exchange the figure of John for the figure of him baptizing someone. Put it over the water shape.* **Many people were excited; they thought that John might be the Christ, the Messiah who was promised by God. John answered their thoughts and said, "I tell you the truth, I am not the Christ. I baptize you with water but another man will come later and baptize you with the Holy Spirit and with fire. I tell you the truth, that man is much better than me. He is God's Son."** *Remove the baptizing shape. Put up the John shape.*

One day, Jesus came to the river. *Add Jesus shape.* **John looked at Jesus and gave this testimony (that means that he spoke only true words): "I saw the spirit of the Lord come down from heaven like a bird, a white dove."** *Place the bird shape on Jesus.* **"The dove landed on Jesus and stayed on him. This sign from God tells me that Jesus is the Christ, the Son of God."**

Jesus said, "John, please baptize Me with water." John said, "I tell you the truth, You should baptize me instead." Jesus answered, "In God's Word, it says that I must be baptized. We must do what God's Word says."

John agreed. He said, "God's Word is the truth, and we must always tell the truth. Let me baptize You now." And so John baptized Jesus. *Put up the shape of John baptizing someone.*

Bible Memory Verse

The Lord hates ... a lying tongue.

Proverbs 6:16–17 (NIV)

Tell the Truth Rubs

Tell the Truth Rubs

Truthful Pictures

Truthful Pictures

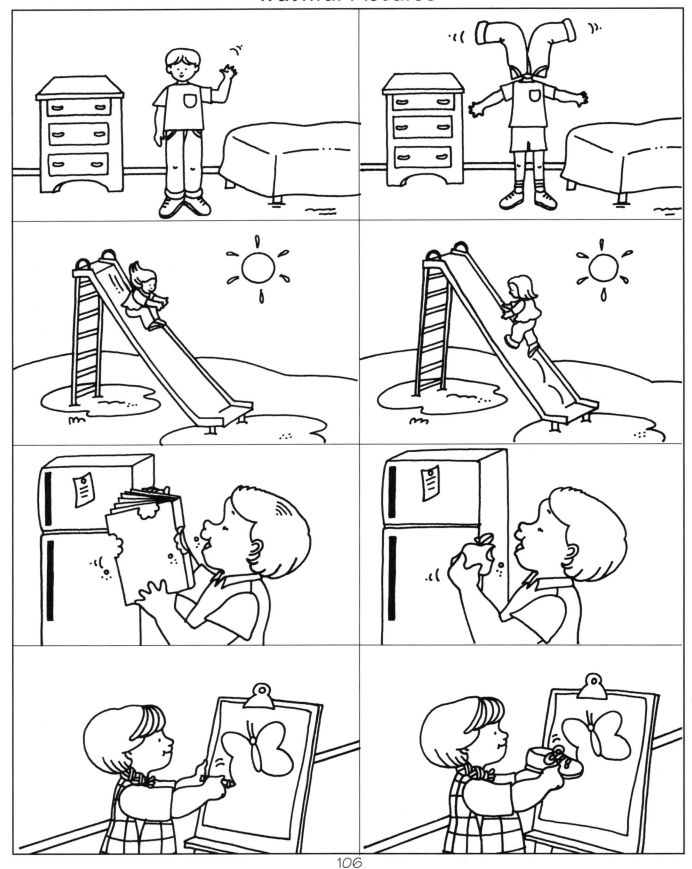

Truthful Pictures

Lying Tongues

The Lord hates ... a lying tongue.
Proverbs 6:16–17 (NIV)

The Lord hates ... a lying tongue.
Proverbs 6:16–17 (NIV)

The Lord hates ... a lying tongue.
Proverbs 6:16–17 (NIV)

The Lord hates ... a lying tongue.
Proverbs 6:16–17 (NIV)

The Lord hates ... a lying tongue.
Proverbs 6:16–17 (NIV)

The Lord hates ... a lying tongue.
Proverbs 6:16–17 (NIV)

Dear Parent(s),

"Tell the truth." You want your child to be truthful. To refrain from lying, to do what is right, to be open and honest with his thoughts and feelings, and to tell others the truth about his faith in Christ. The preschool years are the time to plant the seeds of truthfulness, to water and nurture them. But you will have to be patient—children can't really understand truth and lies until elementary school.

This month our class will learn how John the Baptist spoke the truth—the truth about Christ our Savior. Learning to be truthful and to share the truth of God's Word with others shouldn't stop at the classroom door. I invite you to share this lesson with your child at home by reading the story of John the Baptist from a preschool Bible, trying the activities suggested in this letter, and learning this Bible memory verse.

The Lord hates ... a lying tongue. *Proverbs 6:16–17*

The way children lie, and the reasons they do so, change as they grow. As preschoolers, their thoughts and words are a mixture of fantasy, desire, misunderstanding, and a desire to please others while not getting into trouble themselves. You can help your child "speak the truth" and establish early patterns that discourage lying by understanding how children learn to tell the truth at different stages of development.

How Children Learn to Tell the Truth

Age 3: 3-year-olds rarely lie to deceive, but they may tell quite a few untruths. Your 3-year-old has a vivid imagination and may tell fantastic stories that certainly are not true but neither are they lies. When your child tells you that the pet rabbit at preschool can talk, you might say, "We know rabbits can't really talk, but wouldn't it be fun if they could?" You can help him separate fantasy from reality while still encouraging his creative imagination. Sometimes 3-year-olds lie to test rules. Your child says he didn't ride his trike into the street to see if you will enforce the "stay on the sidewalk" rule. You can firmly state that you know he broke the rule and now must lose his trike-riding privilege for the rest of the morning. This teaches him that you know he broke a rule, that you consistently enforce rules, and that what he did was wrong, without confusing him with the concept of lying. This is a good age to give praise for telling the truth rather than focusing on lies. 3-year-olds will often come and tell you that they have broken a rule or caused an accident. When he tells you that he has spilled the milk, react calmly, help him clean it up, and tell him that you appreciate his truthfulness. He will learn to trust you and be more likely to tell you the truth as he grows up.

Age 4: 4-year-olds still have trouble telling fact from fiction and may tell a lie because they wish something were true. "I didn't break the vase" means "I didn't mean for it to get broken and I wish it hadn't happened." You can help your 4-year-old learn to tell the truth by asking questions that encourage truthfulness. When you know she broke the vase, you can say, "You were bouncing your ball in the house and the ball hit the vase. Now it's broken." Teach her about honesty by being honest yourself. Tell her the truth, "The shot will hurt a little but it will be over quickly," rather than lying to gain her cooperation.

Age 5: 5-year-olds try to tell the truth but aren't always successful. Your 5-year-old will lie to protect himself from punishment. You can help your 5-year-old tell the truth by making it easy to admit wrongdoing. Avoid setting him up to lie by asking, "Did you eat the cake?" Tell him, "I know you ate the cake, it makes me sad when you disobey, now we can't share the cake with your friends." Listen to your child, let him explain the reasons behind his actions. If you understand why he did something wrong, you can help him solve problems in better ways. If he knows that you take the time to listen and care, he is less likely to lie and hide what he did wrong.

Parent's Prayer

Heavenly Father, John spoke the truth—the truth about Christ our Savior. Each day I have the opportunity to teach Your truth to my child just as John taught your truths to the crowds at the river. Please guide me as I teach Your Word and teach about truth by my example. Keep my tongue from telling little lies of convenience, answering questions less than truthfully, and asking others to lie on my behalf. I need Your help to walk a straight path and guide my child away from crooked roads. In Jesus' name I pray. Amen.

Together in Christ,

Family Activities

John's Gelatin Roll-Ups: A Cooking Adventure

Ingredients

- 1 packet unflavored gelatin
- 3 ounces unsweetened juice concentrate, any flavor
- 1 cup boiling water
- 1 ½ cups mini-marshmallows
- Cooking spray

Materials Needed

- 9" × 9" pan
- Whisk
- Medium microwavable bowl
- Wooden spoon
- Sharp knife
- Tall glass

What to Do

1. Spray the bottom and sides of the pan with cooking spray.

2. Follow packet directions to dissolve gelatin in boiling water.

3. Add the marshmallows. Microwave approximately 1 minute or until the marshmallows are puffed and almost melted. Stir gently until the marshmallows are completely melted and the mixture is smooth.

4. Pour into the greased pan. Refrigerate 45 minutes or until set. A creamy layer will rise to the top.

5. Loosen the edges with the knife. Starting at one edge, roll up as tightly as possible. Remove from the pan. Place on a cutting surface with the seam side down.

6. Fill the tall glass with warm water. Dip the sharp knife into the water. Cut into ½" slices. Serve immediately or refrigerate until ready to serve.

Teaching Honesty

• Show your child how you combine the gelatin and marshmallows. Be sure to tell her that they will form two layers when cool—that's the truth! When the gelatin is cool, be sure to show your child the two layers.

• The snack can be eaten rolled up or unrolled. Talk about how this can represent the curved paths and the straight paths that John talked about.

Our Family Tree: A Quiet-Time Activity

Materials Needed

• Photographs of family members (mom, dad, brother, sister, grandparents, cousins, etc.)

• Large piece of paper or poster board

• Marker

• Tape or glue

What to Do

Without your child:

1. Assemble all the needed materials.

2. Use the photographs to make a family tree picture. Tape or glue them to the large sheet of paper, writing their names and relationship to the child underneath the photos.

3. Draw a tree with trunk and branches around the family photos.

With your child:

1. Name each of the people on the family tree. Talk about how that person is related to the child.

2. Leave the family tree where the child can see it. When you speak of an absent family member, such as a grandparent who lives far away, point out his or her picture to your child.

Teaching Honesty

• Be aware that your child may have difficulty understanding that the relative has more than one family role. Tell him the truth, people can have many roles in the family (brother, father, son, and uncle) all at the same time. Patiently explain again and again that his uncle is your brother.

• Be honest with your child. Tell him that the exact relationship between Mary and Elizabeth (and thus between Jesus and John) is unknown. All that we know for sure is that they were kinswomen (Luke 1:36).

- Family was important to Jesus' ministry. John heralded the coming of Jesus; the miracle of changing water into wine happened at a relative's wedding. Help your child to understand that even today, family is important and God can do great things in your family.

Our Baptismal Font: Taking a Trip

Materials Needed

- Permission to visit your church during the week.

What to Do

1. Call your church office and ask about a convenient time to visit the sanctuary during the week. Ask whether there are any areas that are off-limits during your visit.

2. Take your child on a midweek trip to visit the baptismal font at church. Take time to explore the font, as well as other parts of the church that he might not experience during the regular church service.

Teaching Honesty

- Talk about how the water is used. Explain that some churches baptize adults and some baptize children. Describe how it is done: full submersion or sprinkling. Explain that different churches baptize differently. Be honest: Share your belief and faith.

- Tell your child about the Baptism service. If your church has an established service for Baptism, ask for a copy of the service. Read some of the words to your child and explain what they mean.

- Tell your child a story about your own Baptism and your child's Baptism. Help her understand how powerful this experience is. Ask her how she thinks Jesus might have felt when she was baptized.

- Your child may appear disinterested in the baptismal font and everything that you are trying to share with her. In all honesty, she may be more interested in climbing on and off the pews. Be assured that she does hear some of what you are saying. Have faith that you have laid a foundation for discussion of Baptism at a later date.

Easy Stuff

1. When your child takes a bath and plays with toys in the water, talk about how Jesus washed away our sins in Baptism.

2. Watch birds fly and talk about how the Holy Spirit, in the form of a dove, flew down onto Jesus.

3. Use books, TV programs, and conversations heard to identify truths and lies. If a person has lied, ask your child what the person should have done differently to be honest.